Belleville Ontario Book 3 in Colour Photos, Saving Our History One Photo at a Time

Photography
by Barbara Raué
2016

Series Name:
Cruising Ontario

Book 165: Belleville Book 3

Cover photo: 257 Bridge Street East, Page 16

Series Name: Cruising Ontario
Saving Our History One Photo at a Time
in colour photos

Books Available in Alphabetical Order:
Aberfoyle, Acton, Alton, Amherstburg, Ancaster, Arthur, Aylmer, Ayr, Bloomingdale, Brantford, Burlington, Caledon, Caledonia, Cambridge, Clifford, Conestogo, Delhi, Dorchester to Aylmer, Drayton, Drumbo, Dundas, Eden Mills, Elmira, Elora, Essex, Fergus, Guelph, Hagersville, Hamilton, Hanover, Harriston, Hespeler, Jarvis, Kingston, Kingsville, Kitchener, Linwood, Listowel, London, Lucknow, Mono, Mount Forest, Neustadt, New Hamburg, Niagara-on-the-Lake, Oakville, Orangeville, Orillia, Owen Sound, Palmerston, Peterborough, Petrolia, Port Elgin, Preston, Rockwood, Sarnia, Seaforth, Sheffield, Shelburne, Simcoe, Southampton, St. Jacobs, St. Marys, St. Thomas, Stoney Creek, Stratford, Thamesford, Tillsonburg, Waterdown, Waterford, Waterloo, Welland, Wellesley, Windsor, Wingham, Woodstock

Other Books by Barbara Raue

Coins of Gold

Arrows, Indians and Love

The Life and Times of Barbara
Volume 1: Inventions That Have Enhanced My Life
Volume 2: Entertainment That I Have Enjoyed
Volume 3: East Coast Trips
Volume 4: Olympics Have Always Intrigued Me
Volume 5: Wonders of the World
Volume 6: Caribbean Cruises We Have Enjoyed
Volume 7: Animals
Volume 8: Storms and Other Major Disasters in My Lifetime
Volume 9: Wars, Terrorist Attacks and Major Disasters

The Cromwell Family Book

Laura Secord Discovered

Daddy Where Are You?

Montana Series
Book 1: Montana Dream
Book 2: Life on the Montana Frontier
Book 3: Montana to Boston and Back

Visit Barbara's website to view all of her books
http://barbararaue.ca

Table of Contents

Belleville is a city located at the mouth of the Moira River on the Bay of Quinte in southeastern Ontario. It was the site of a Mississaugas' village in the eighteenth century. It was settled by United Empire Loyalists beginning in 1784. It was named Belleville in honor of Lady Arabella Gore in 1816, after a visit to the settlement by Sir Francis Gore and his wife.

It is known as the "friendly city" because it offers big city amenities along with small town friendliness, and a pleasing mixture of the historic and modern.

Belleville became an important railway junction with the completion of the Grand Trunk Railway in 1855. In 1858 the iron bridge over the Moira River at Bridge Street was constructed. Belleville's beautiful High Victorian Gothic city hall was built in 1872 to house the public market and administrative offices.

Due to its location near Lake Ontario, its climate is moderated by cooling hot summer days and warming cold days during the fall and winter.

Procter & Gamble, Kellogg's, Redpath, and Sears are corporations operating in Belleville. There are many other manufacturing sector companies which operate within the City of Belleville, including Sprague Foods, Sigma Stretch Film Canada, Reid's Dairy, and Parmalat Canada - Black Diamond Cheese Division, to name a few.

Belleville has an excellent yacht harbor, which is a picturesque stopping point for Great Lakes sailors and a favorite launch for sports fishing enthusiasts after walleye, pike and bass. Beautiful music chimes can be heard all year long from the City Hall clock tower, overlooking the new civic square and Farmers Market. Walking, biking and rollerblading can be enjoyed on the Bayshore and Riverfront Trails.

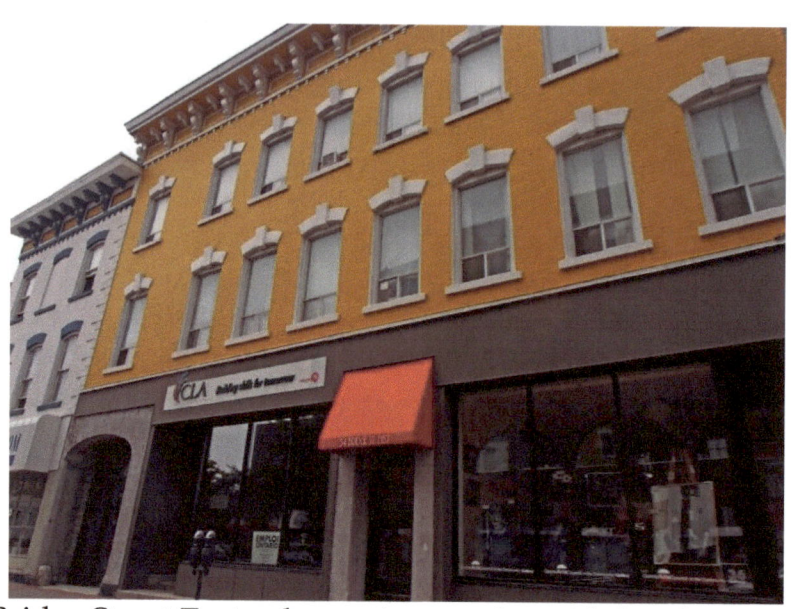

34 Bridge Street East – decorative cornice with brackets, corner quoins on far building

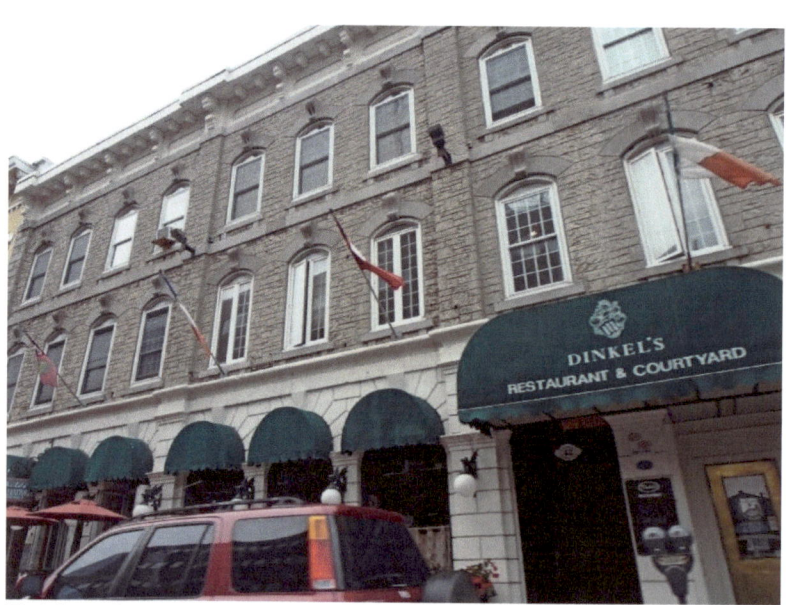

44 Bridge Street East – Dinkel's Restaurant and Courtyard – stone, cornice brackets, pilasters, courses

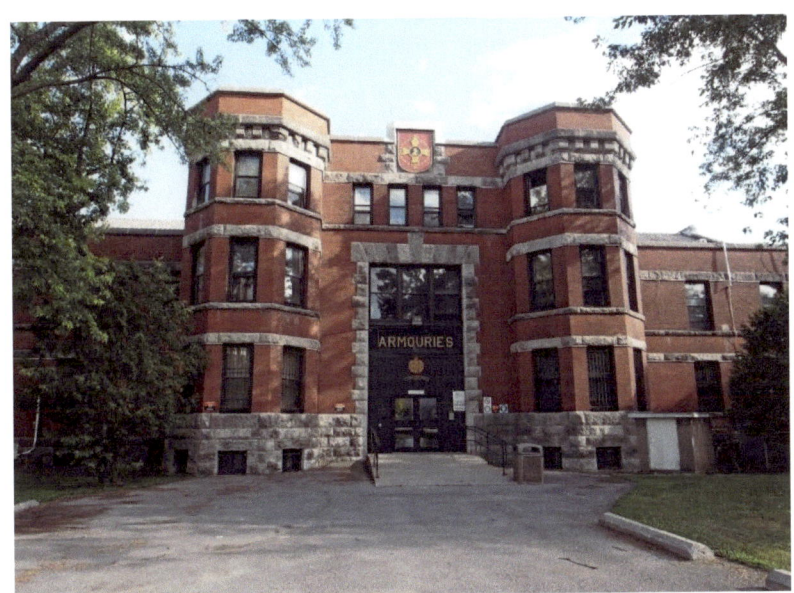

Bridge Street East - Belleville Armouries - The structure brings to mind a medieval fortress as evidenced in the solid brick construction, stone detailing and the use of three-storey towers flanking the entrance of the administrative block. It has a symmetrically organized façade with rough-cut stone window dressings, narrow vertical window openings, and its medieval detailing such as the string courses, copings and battlements.

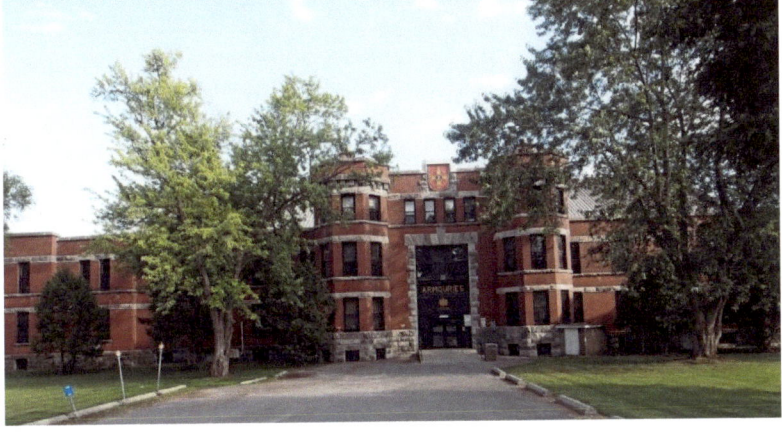

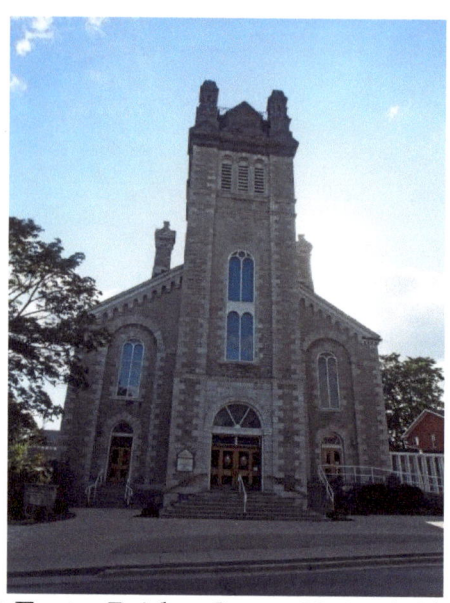

60 Bridge Street East – Bridge Street United Church of Canada – built 1887 – Romanesque style, rounded windows with muntins, bevelled dentil molding, quoining, pediments on tower with decorated tympanums, rose window on the side

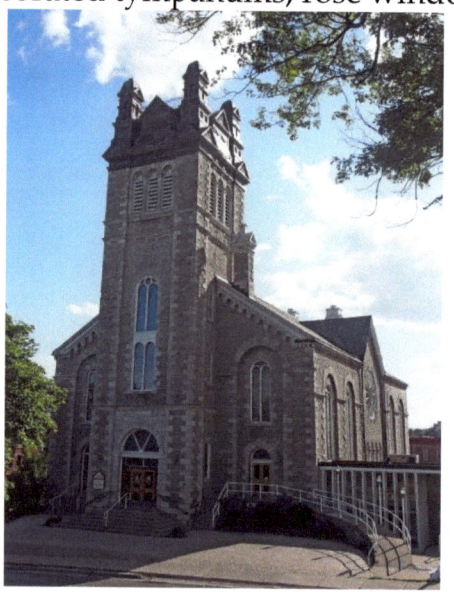

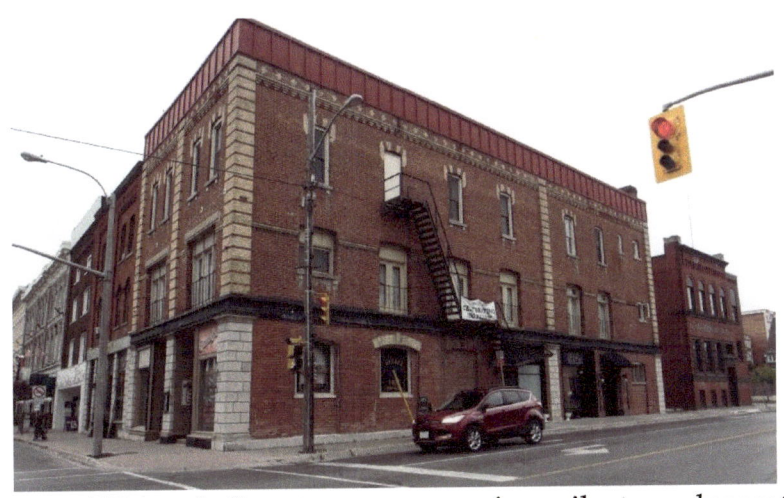

Corner of Pinnacle Street – corner quoins, pilasters, decorative cornice, bevelled dentil molding

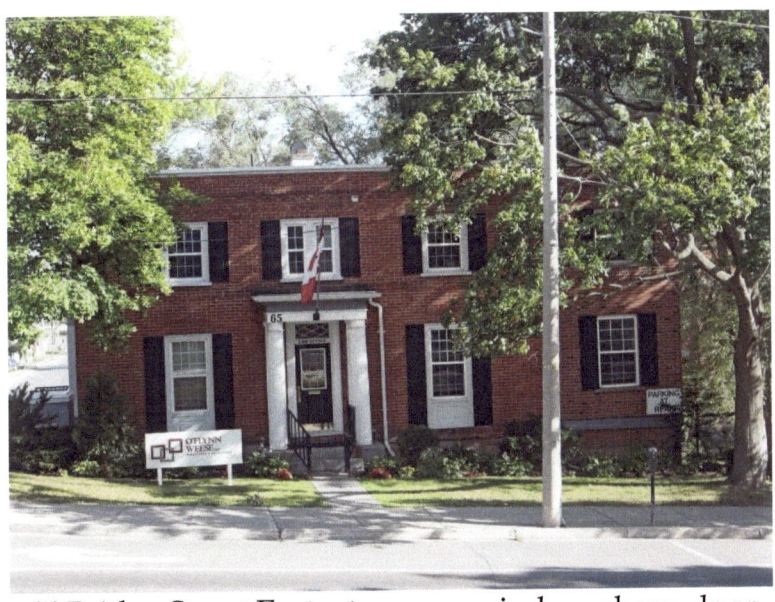

65 Bridge Street East – transom window above door

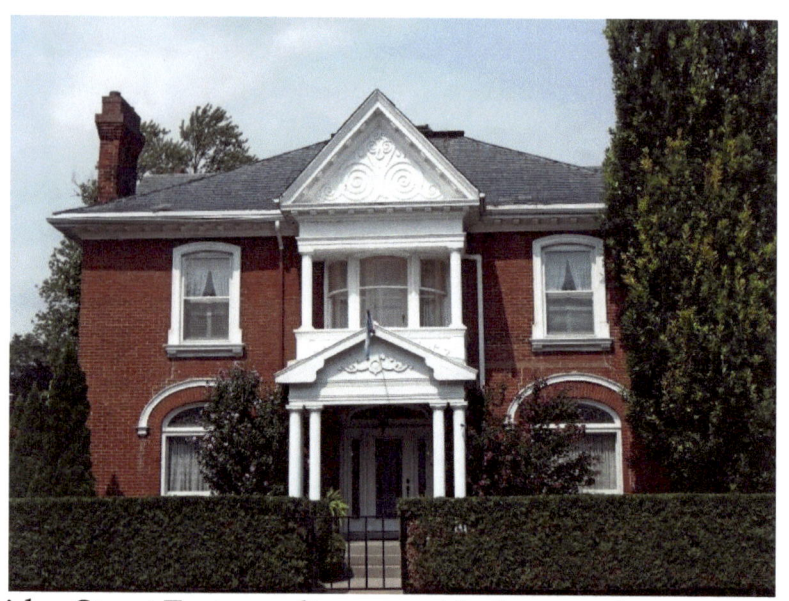

Bridge Street East – pediments with decorated tympanums, hipped roof, Doric pillars

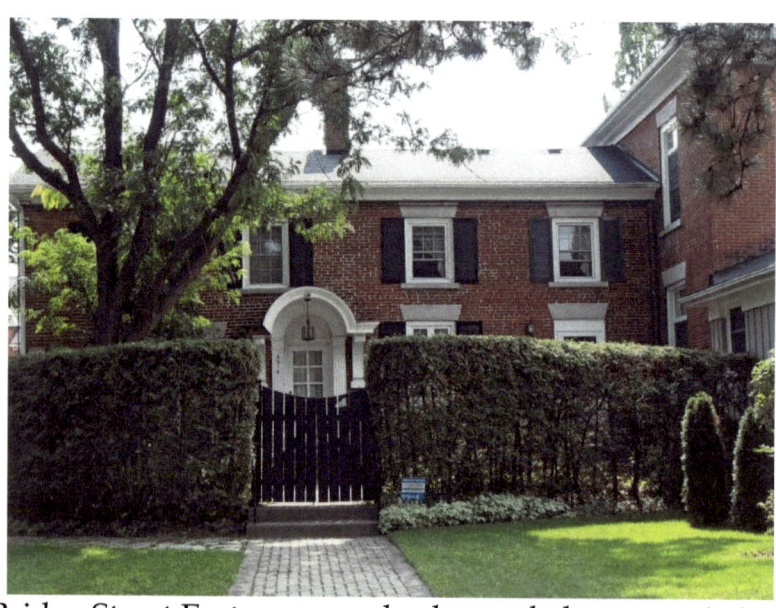

99 Bridge Street East – engaged columns below a semi-circular pediment

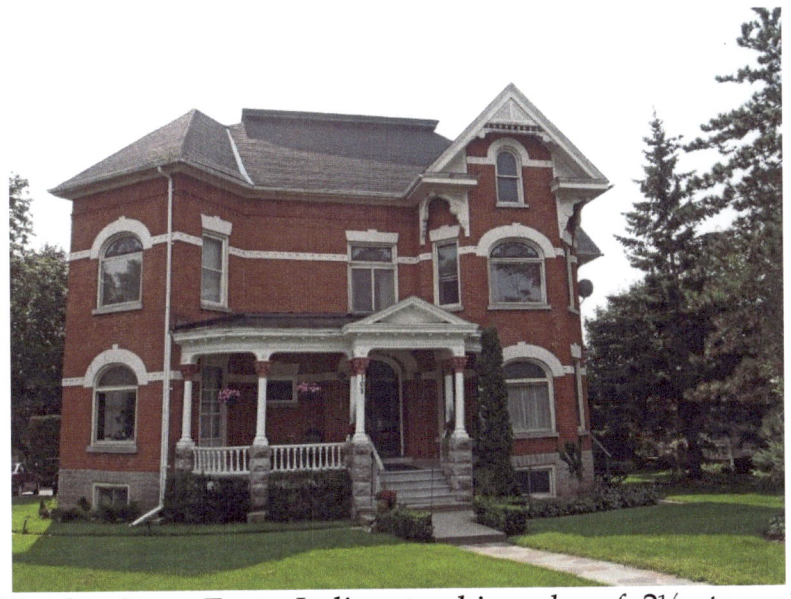

105 Bridge Street East – Italianate - hipped roof, 2½-storey bay
with cornice return on gable, banding, Corinthian pillars on
veranda, pediment

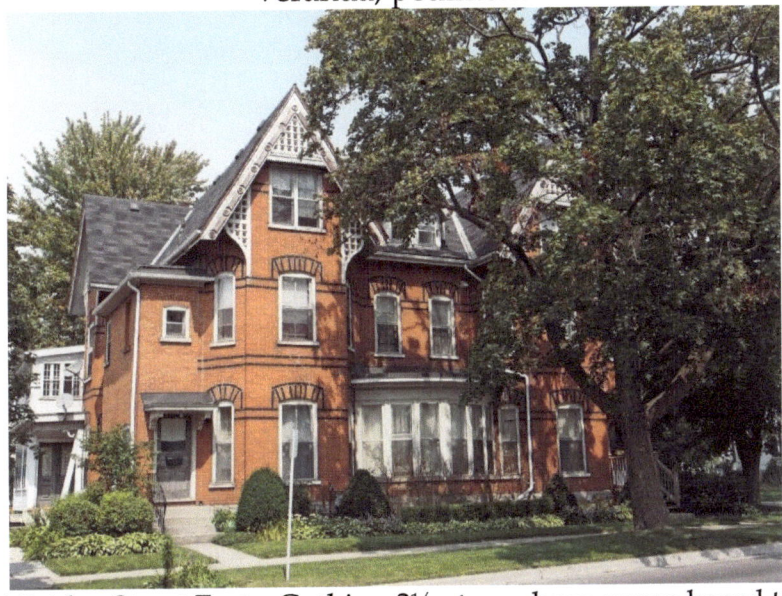

114 Bridge Street East – Gothic – 2½-storey bays, verge board trim
and fretwork on gables, dichromatic banding and voussoirs

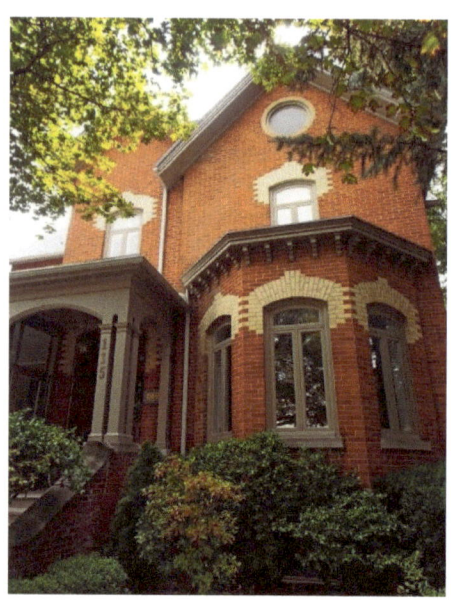

115 Bridge Street East – dichromatic brickwork, bay window with brackets

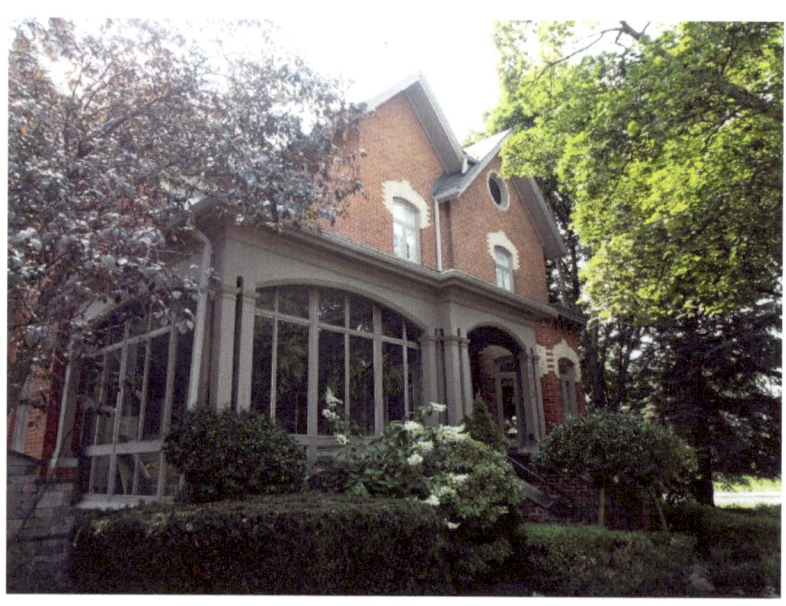

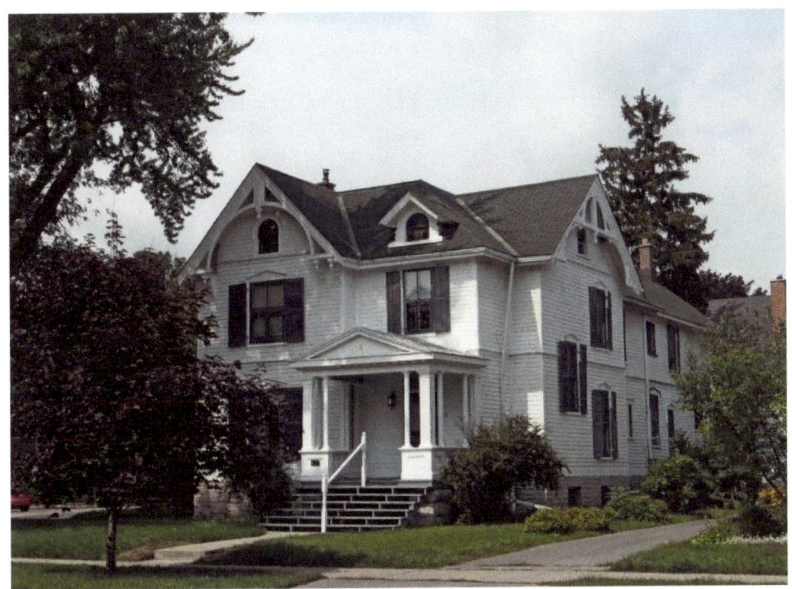

118 Bridge Street East - **built** in 1895 by Mr. H. Pringle of the Pringle Company, Belleville – builders specializing in hardwood interior fittings – 2½-storey clapboard on original stone foundation; façades with peaked gables and bargeboard with a design typical of the time; windows have decorative trim, shutters and pedimented heads

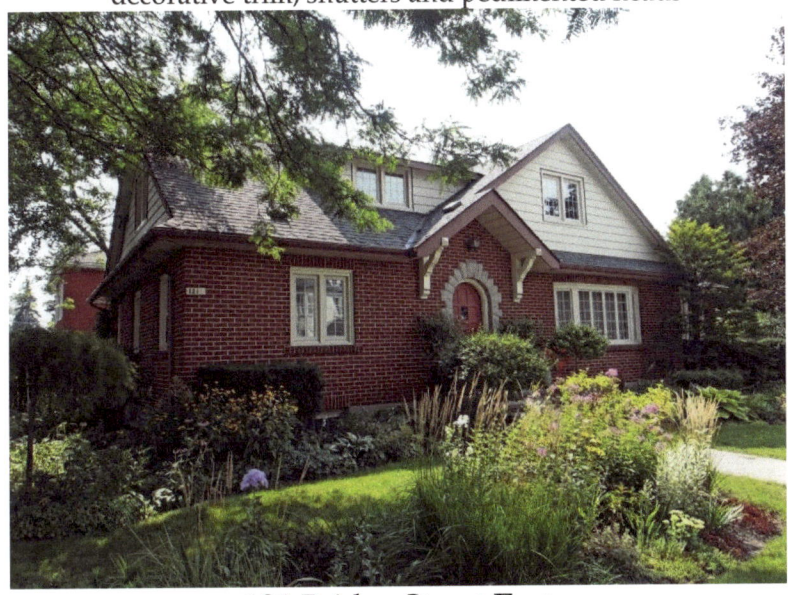

121 Bridge Street East

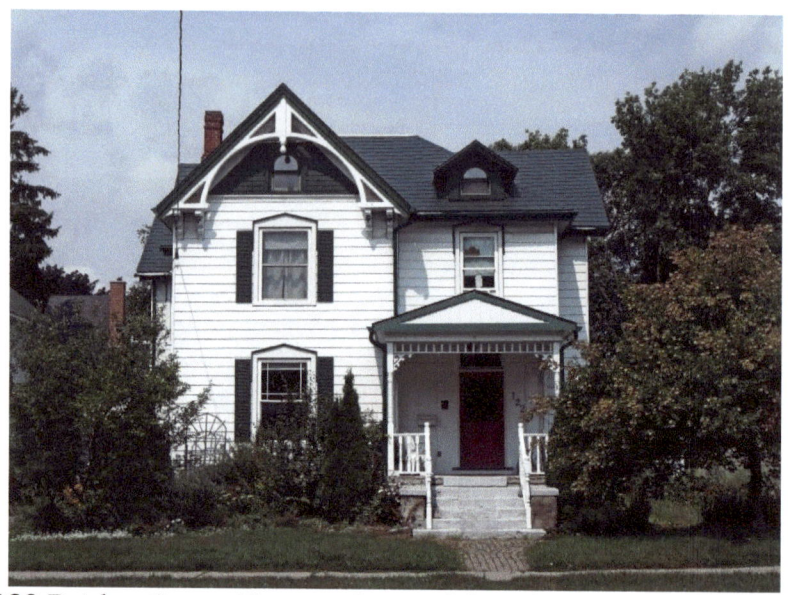

122 Bridge Street East – trim and finial on gable, dormer, pediment, decorative capitals on turned veranda supports with spindling

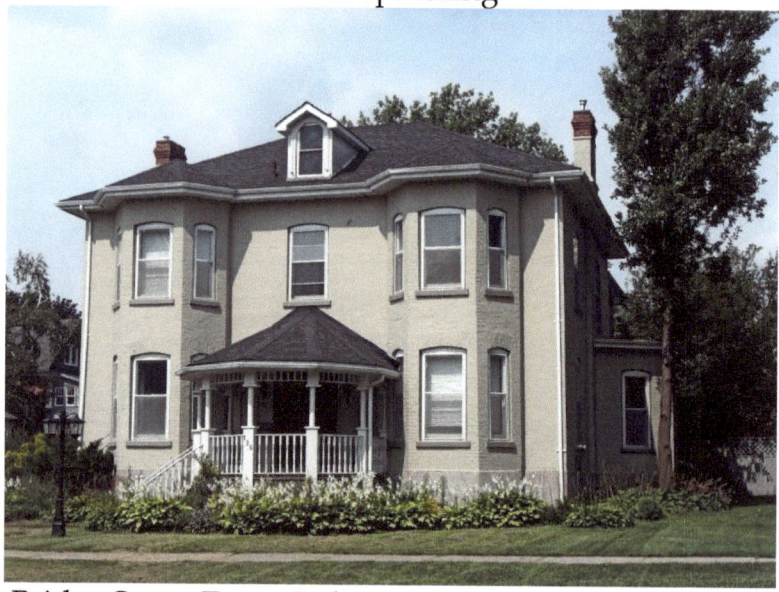

126 Bridge Street East – Italianate – hipped roof with dormer, two-storey bay windows

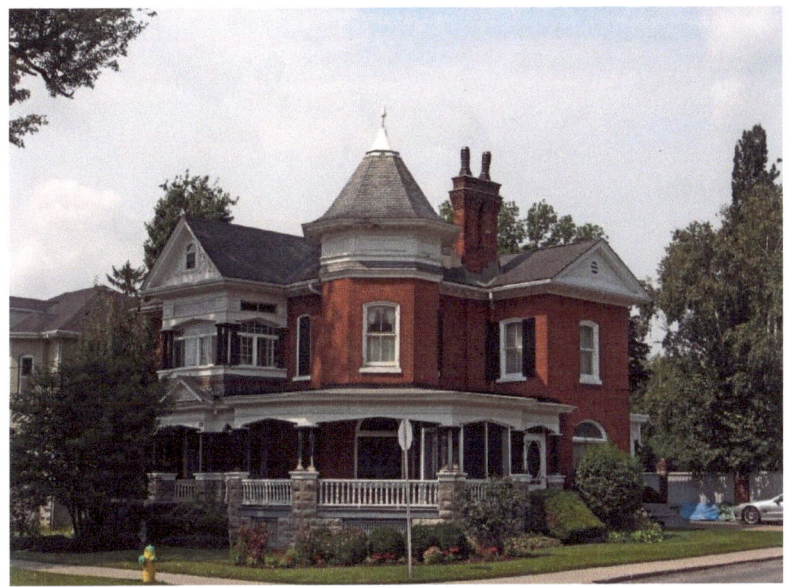

128 Bridge Street East – Queen Anne style – turret, tall decorative chimney, decorative tympanums on the gables, pediment, open railing on the veranda

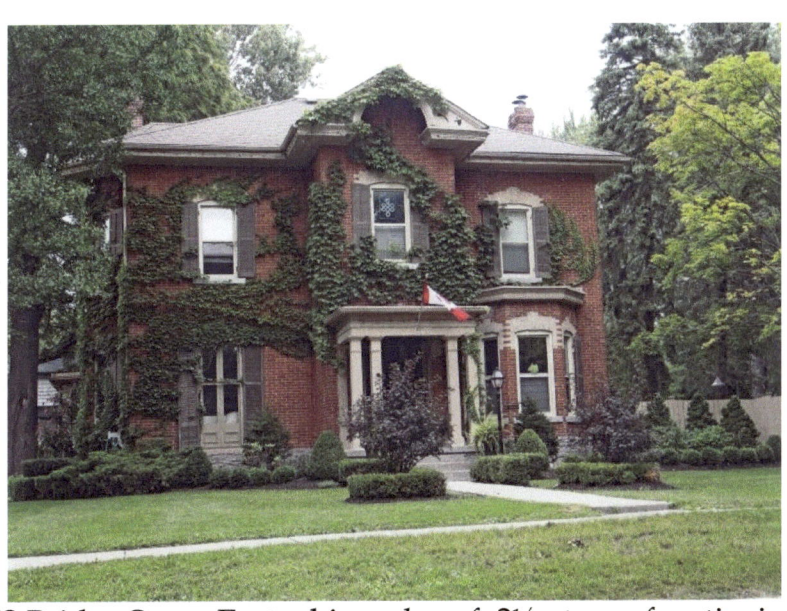

252 Bridge Street East – hipped roof, 2½-storey frontispiece, dichromatic brickwork, bay window

The Phillips-Burrows-Faulknor House
Glanmore National Historic Site
257 Bridge Street East

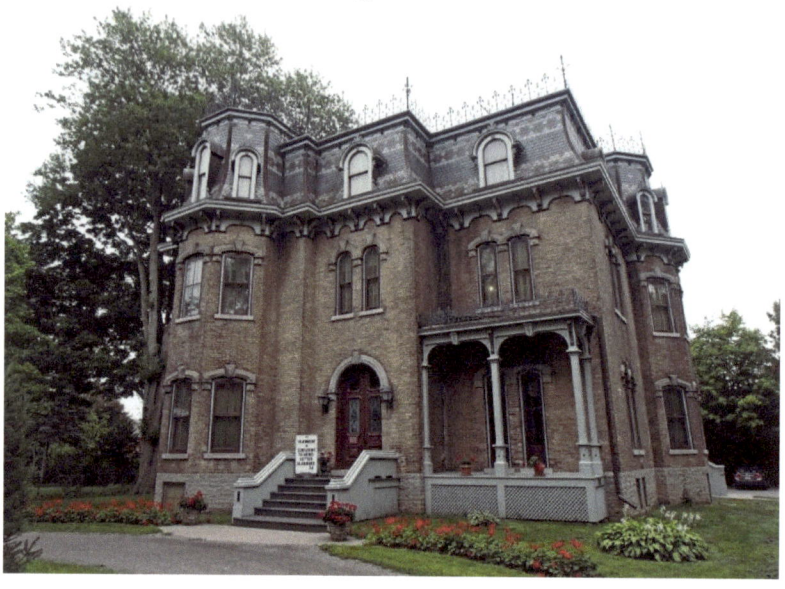

Glanmore's property was originally a block wide and extended to Highway 2 (Dundas Street). Harriet Phillips inherited this property from George Bleecker, her grandfather. Glanmore reflects the tastes of the well-to-do in late nineteenth century Canada. The Mountain Ash, Norway Spruce, flower beds and antique rose garden are restored features of Glanmore's original landscape. The grand house, built by local architect Thomas Hanley, was built in 1882-1883 for wealthy banker John Philpot Curran Phillips and his wife Harriet Ann Dougall, the daughter of Belleville's Judge Benjamin Dougall. It is in the Second Empire style with mansard roof with elaborate cornices and brackets, dormer windows, iron cresting, a built-in gutter system, and multi-colored slate. The polychromatic slates were obtained from quarries in Vermont (green), New York (red), and black from Quebec.

The 9,000 square foot home cost $7,000 to build in 1883. The impressive suspended walnut staircase cost $62.50. The spelter (a zinc alloy) statue lamps and the hanging vigil lamp are displayed in their original locations.

The Reception Room was used to receive callers. In the 19th century, strict etiquette was followed. Visitors upon their arrival presented their calling cards to a servant and then waited in the Reception Room. If the hostess was available, the visitor was shown in. If the hostess was unavailable, then a calling card was left in a card receiver.

The table in the Dining Room with ten leaves, chairs, side board, and fireplace mantle are original to the house. Mr. and Mrs. Phillips hosted elegant dinners in this setting. A bell located behind the far door was used to summon the servants.

The Breakfast Room and Service Hall is an informal room where the family ate casual meals. The speaking tube beside the door to the hall allowed them to contact the servants in the hall below. Servants used the back service hallway which connects this room with the front of the house.

The Billiard and Card Rooms were added to the house sometime after 1900. The reeded paneling and wood accents are a combination of oak, ash and pine. The masculine décor of the Pool Room is complemented by the original pool table, cues, balls, racks, overhead counter and stag-head shelves. The smaller Card Room was used for board and card games. The cloisonné vases on the mantelpiece, the paintings and the Scottish oak sideboard (circa 1850) are from the Couldery Collection.

Bertram and Cecilia Couldery came to Belleville from England in the early 1880s. A train delay resulted in them spending the night at the Docter's Hotel in Belleville. They developed a friendship with the Docter family and made a second home in Belleville. The Coulderys were active painters. Cecilia painted portraits and flowers in a variety of media. Her husband Bertram painted landscapes and copied works of well-known artists such as Rembrandt, Sir Edwin Landseer, John Constable, and Sir David Wilkie. Bertram's older brother Horatio painted animals.

The North Drawing Room was used by Mr. and Mrs. Phillips for entertaining. Ornate columns divide the North and South areas of the double drawing room. The rooms could also be used as a ballroom when the carpets and furniture were removed. The coffered ceilings feature molded ornamental plaster and hand-painted designs. The decorative ceilings are complemented by the original settees, three-seated chaperone's chair, and mantle surround. The clutter of decorative objects is typical of late Victorian style.

The Second Bedroom, originally intended as a guest bedroom, may have been occupied by Jessie Patterson when she came to live at Glanmore in 1896.

The Master Bedroom and Bathroom is an expansive room used by Mr. and Mrs. Phillips. The bell on the wall next to the bed summoned the servants. There are also speaking tubes that enabled Mr. and Mrs. Phillips to speak to the servants in the lower levels. The original bathroom was one of the first in Belleville to be fitted with indoor plumbing, and features a copper-lined tub. A water storage tank above the room collected rain water that was used to supply fixtures with cold water. Additional water was heated downstairs and pumped up to the bathroom.

Hair pictures and hair jewelry dated back centuries and gained popularity in the nineteenth century. Queen Victoria made them popular by occasionally exchanging gifts of hair jewelry with relatives and other heads of state in Europe. Hair pictures were often used as family heirlooms. A piece of hair would be taken from a loved one at an early age or shortly after death and used to begin a picture. Over the years the hair of other family members would be slowly added and the picture expanded perhaps over one hundred years. Hair was also used to craft brooches or kept in lockets as mementos to loved ones.

The Lower Level has not been restored. There are no original photographs and very little information in the original specifications. The West side of the basement originally contained the kitchen, pantry and servants bedroom. The East side contained the furnace room with a wood furnace, and a cistern. Water was collected from the gutters into a tank in the ceiling of the bathroom. The water then flowed through a pipe to the cistern below. Eleanor Bowden, a servant at Glanmore from 1901 to 1905, describes her time there as happy days. Her employers were decent and kind. Eleanor's skill as a maid of all work was highly regarded by John and Harriet Phillips.

Glanmore had seven fireplaces that burned coal or gas which meant that fire tending and its associated tasks were an important and laborious part of the maid's daily routine. Rising at five or six in the morning, the maid's first job was to clean the grates and light the fires, as well as prepare a hot morning beverage for the household. At the end of the day, the maid banked the fires, piling the coals to ensure that the fireplaces would heat the house well into the night.

Maintaining order in a home the size of Glanmore required organization, hard work, and long hours for the domestic staff. The general servant had the responsibility of scrubbing floors and woodwork, beating or sweeping carpets, and washing windows and walls. Daily duties included dusting, making beds and emptying slops. General kitchen duties included making the kitchen ready for the cook and basic food preparation. The maid was expected to clean and scour stew pans, sauce pans, sauté pans, frying pans and all the kitchen utensils. She was also required to wash all dishes and keep the kitchen and scullery clean and in good order. Laundry was an important task in most Victorian households and involved a great deal of heavy work. Washing an entire household's linens and clothes usually required a full day. The following day would be spent folding, mangling, starching, crimping, ironing and mending.

Today the East side of the Lower Level features exhibits on local history. The first exhibit illustrates the lives and activities of the domestic servants who lived and worked at Glanmore during the early 1900s. The exhibit features typical domestic tools and equipment from the period. The second exhibit portrays an early settler homestead with local artifacts dating from the 1850s to the 1880s. During the period that the Phillips family resided at Glanmore, many rural families were still living in homes such as this. There is also a display of local artist Rev. Bowen P. Squire's paintings depicting aspects of Loyalist settlement in the Bay of Quinte region from 1784 to 1850.

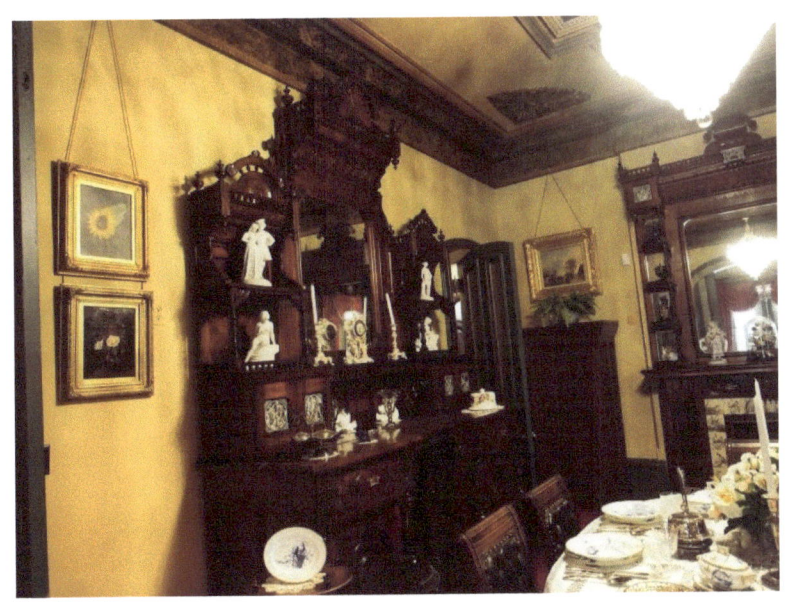

Dining Room

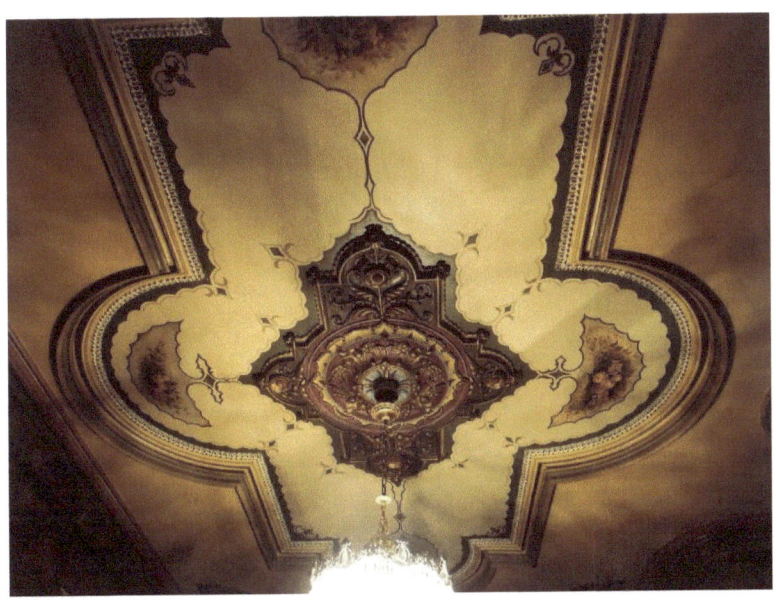

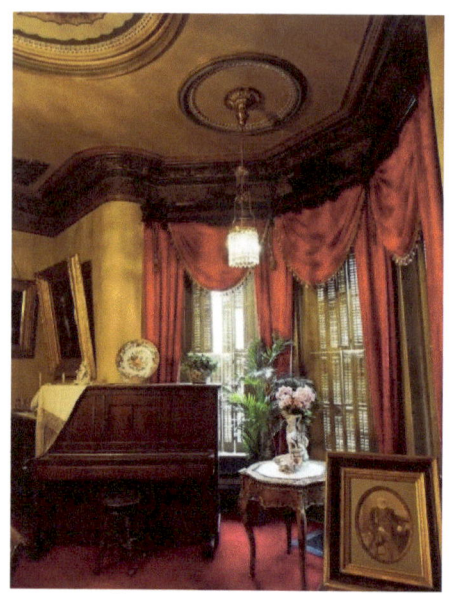

Reception Room

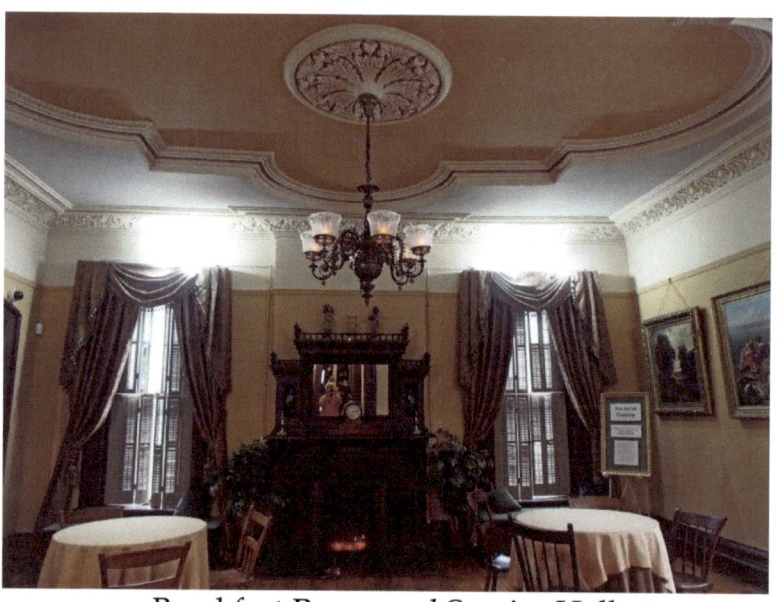

Breakfast Room and Service Hall

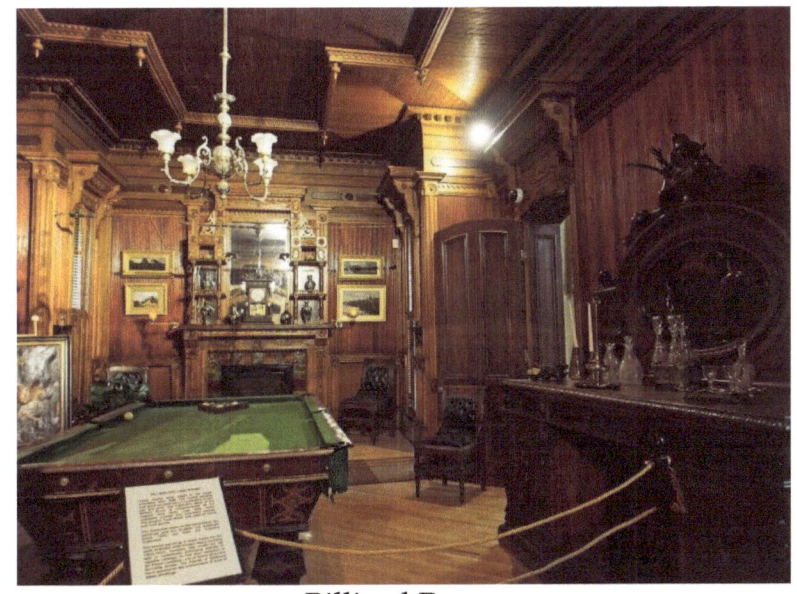

Billiard Room

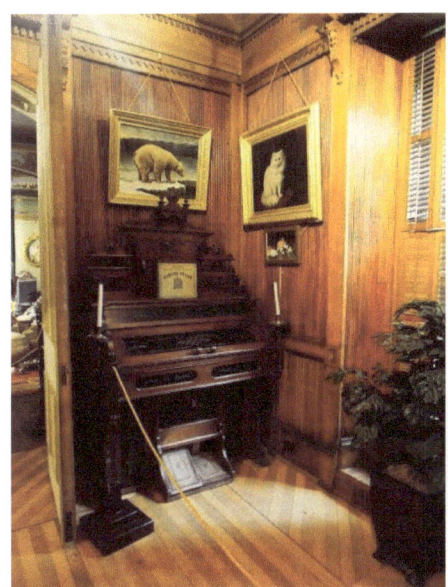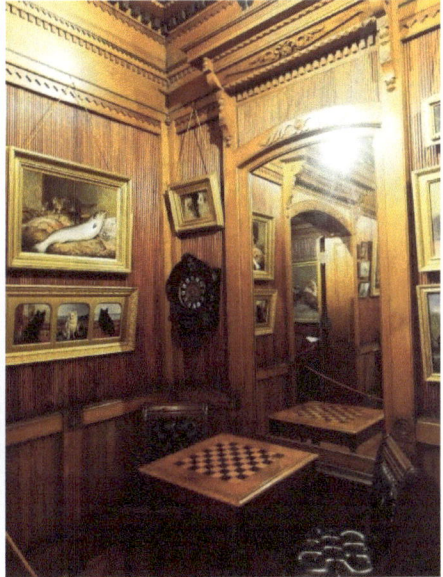

Card Room

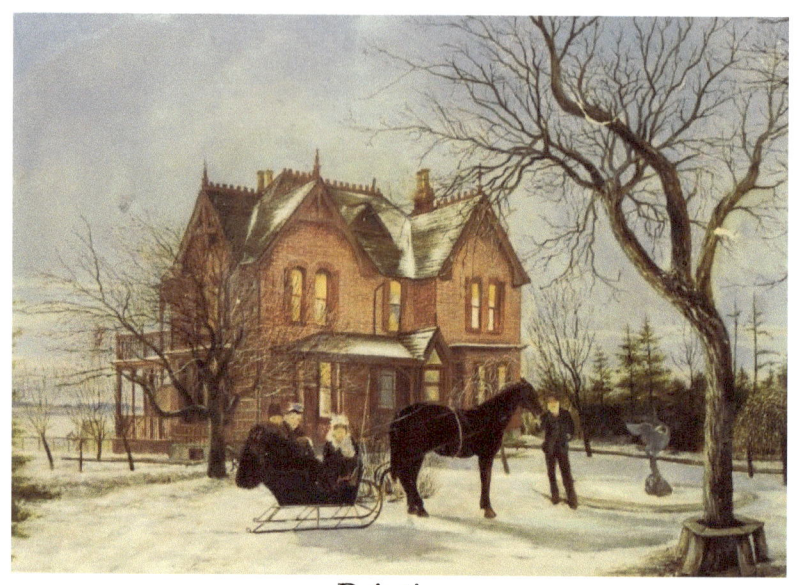

Painting

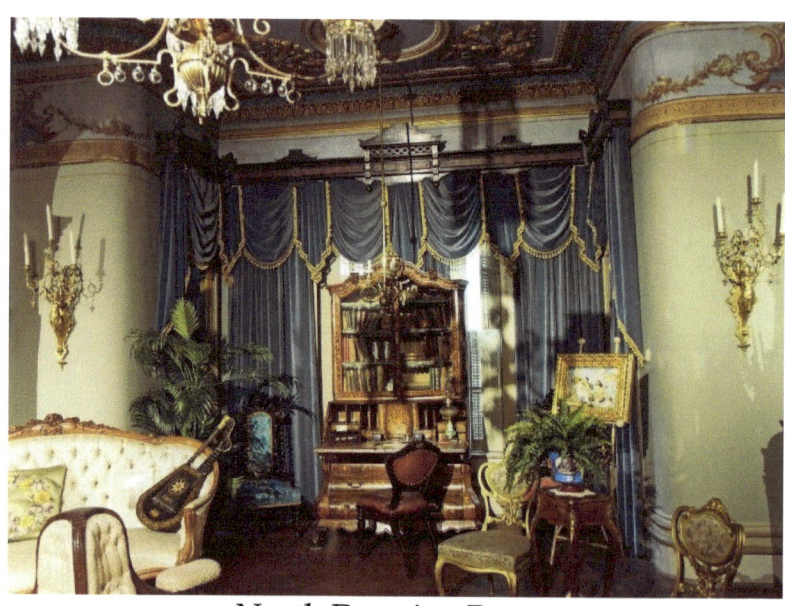

North Drawing Room

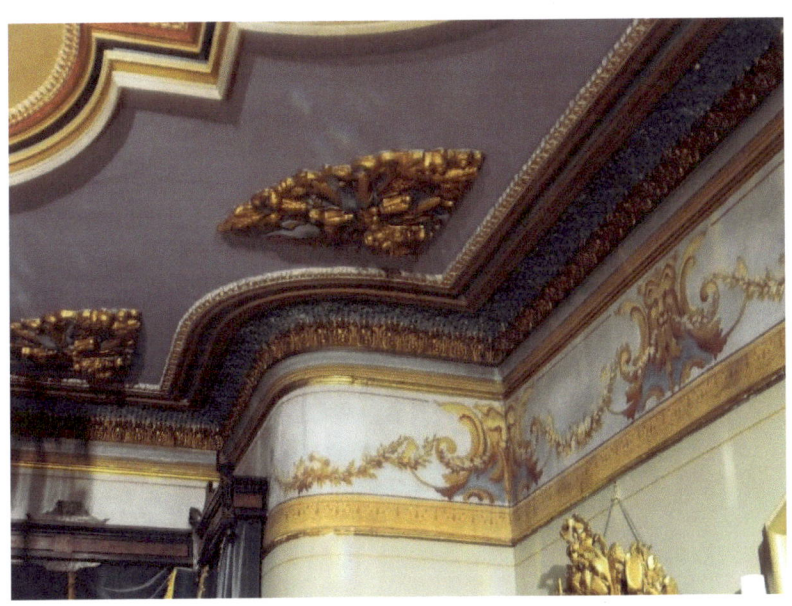

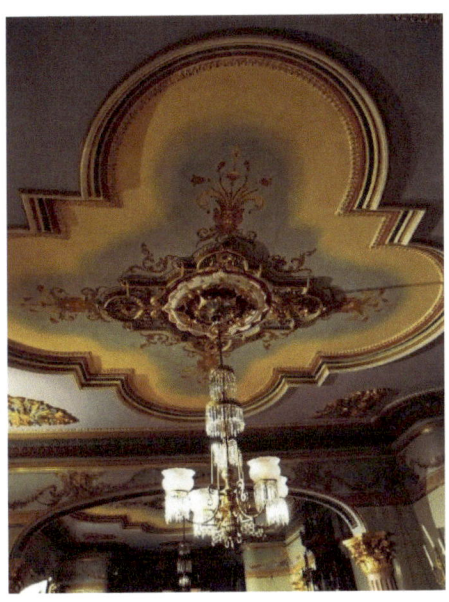

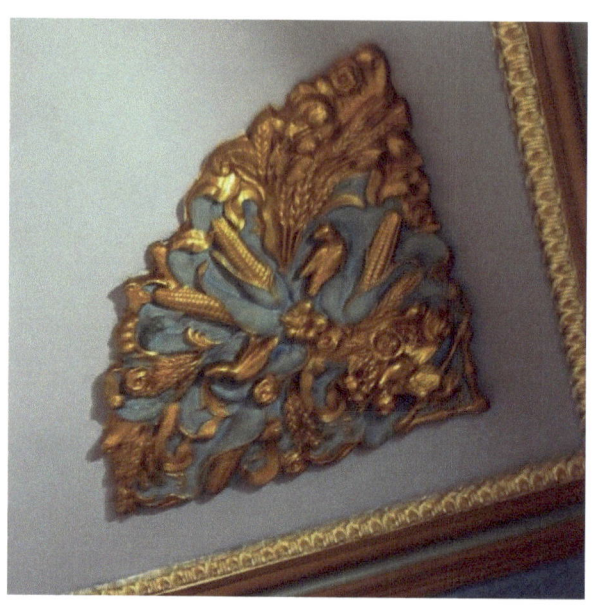

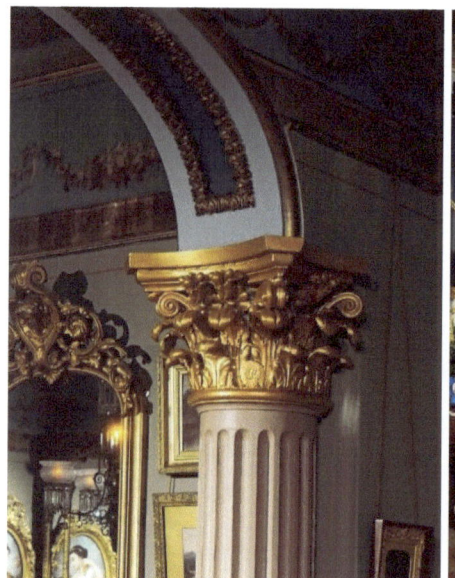

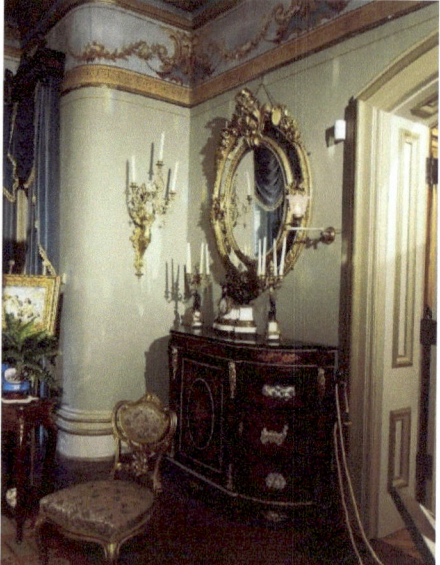

Composite pillars dividing North
and South Drawing Rooms

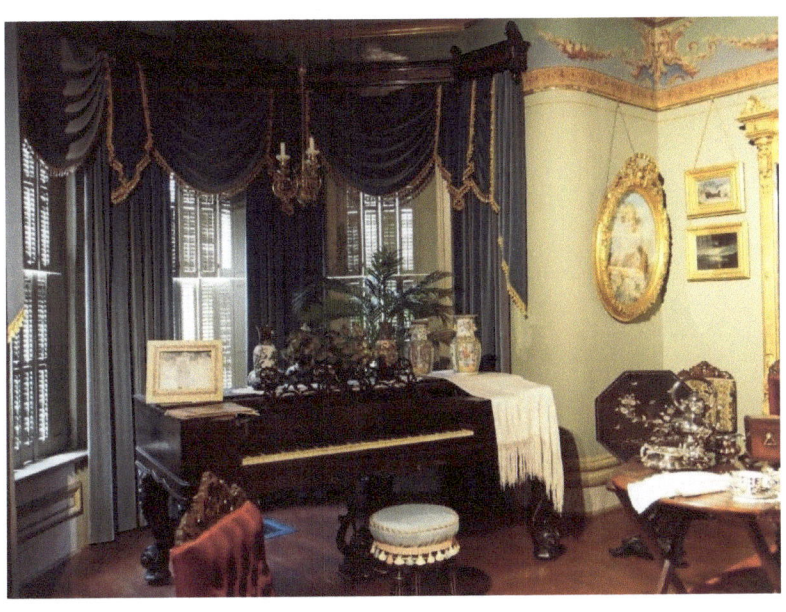

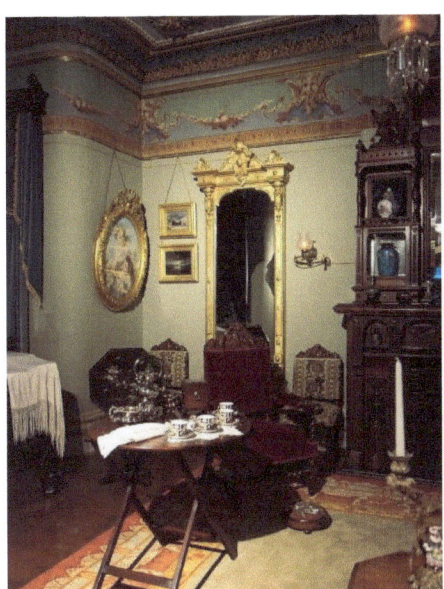

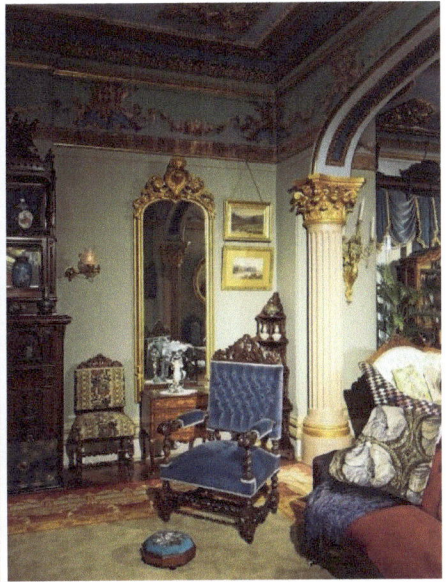

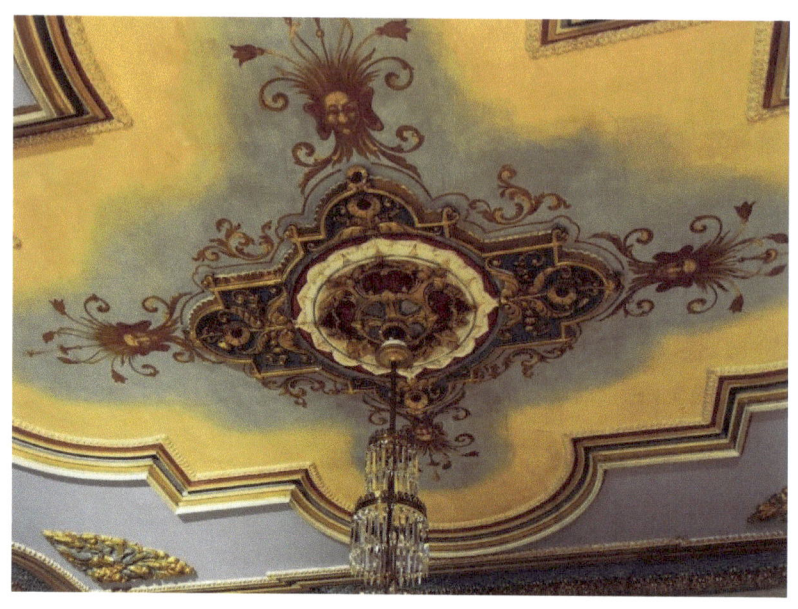

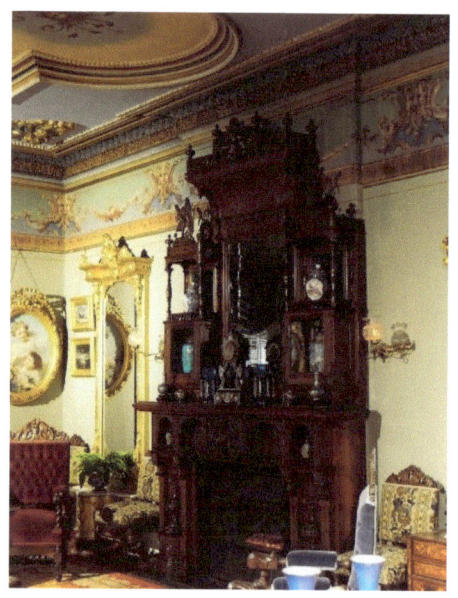

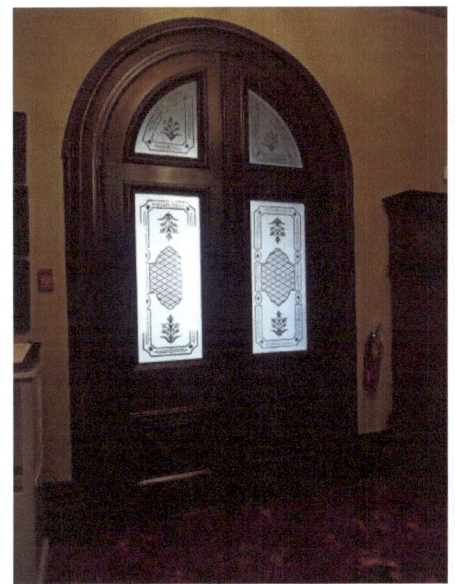

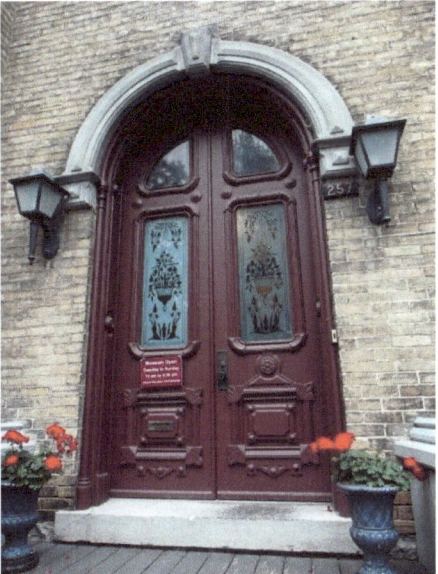

Door from inside   Door from outside

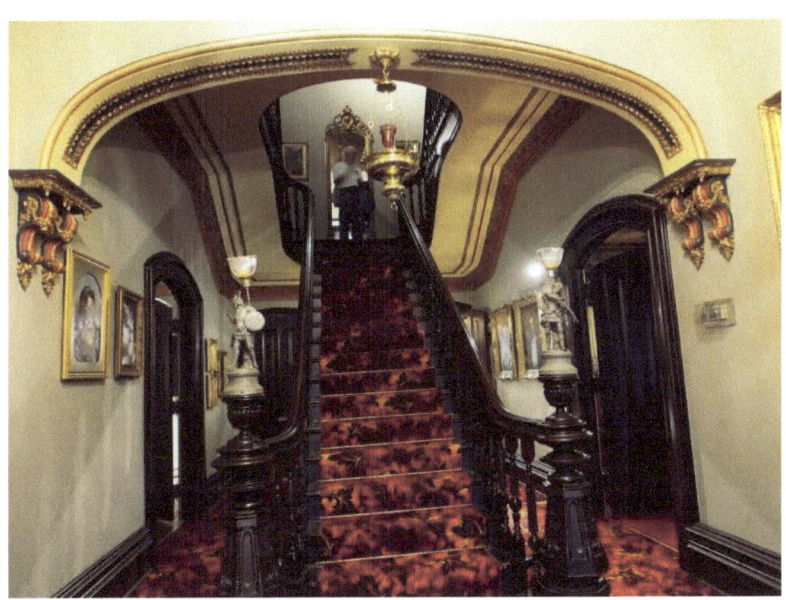

Suspended walnut staircase – hanging vigil lamp

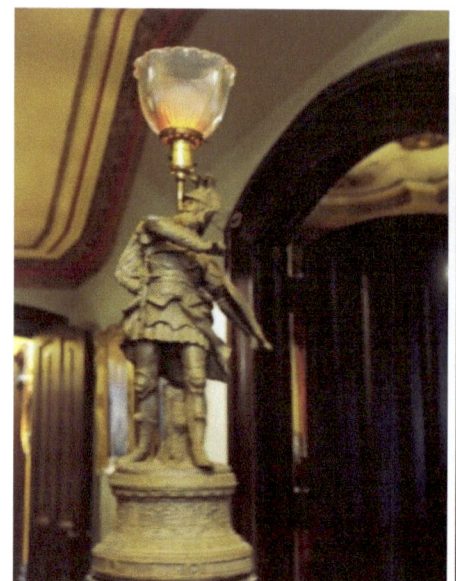
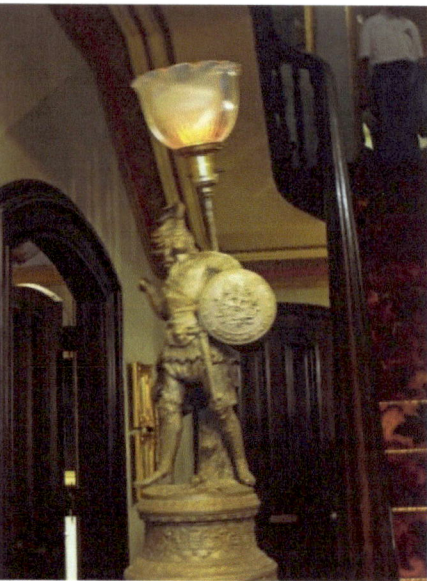

Spelter statue lamps

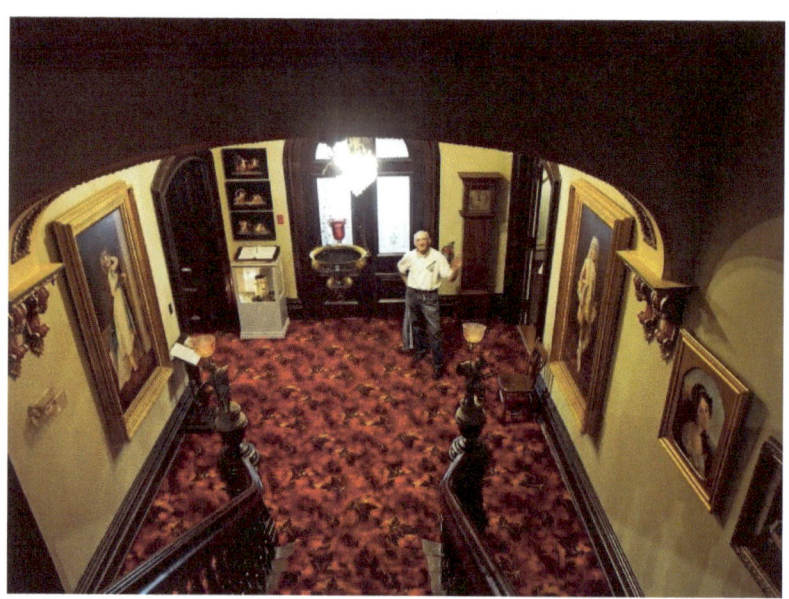

Looking down the staircase

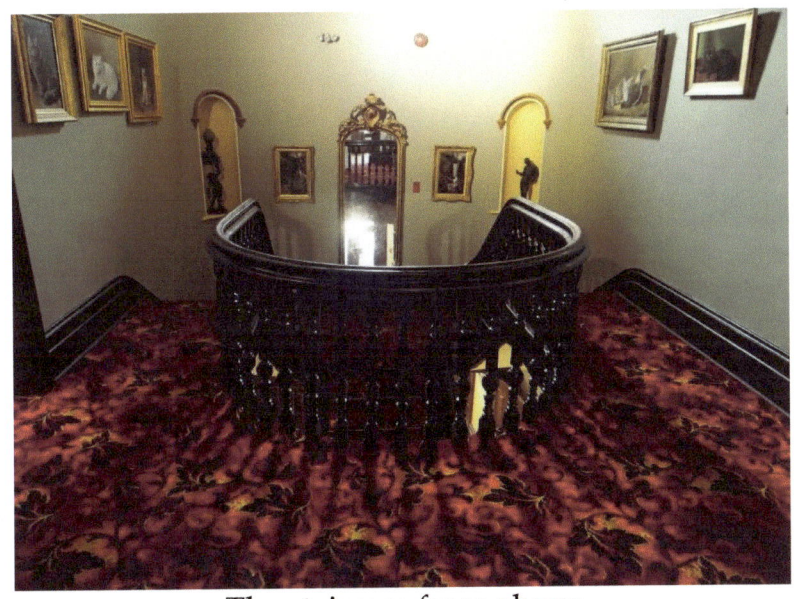

The staircase from above

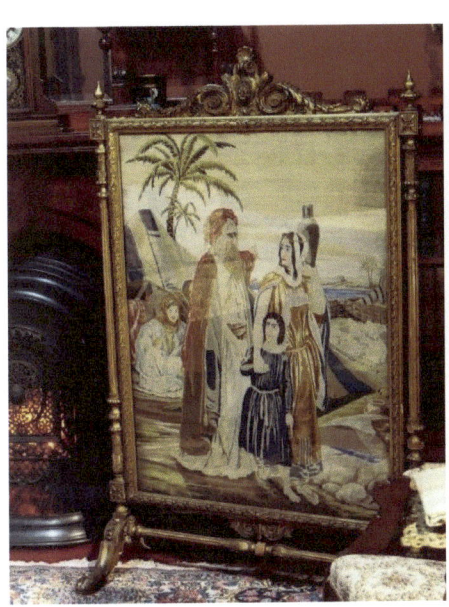

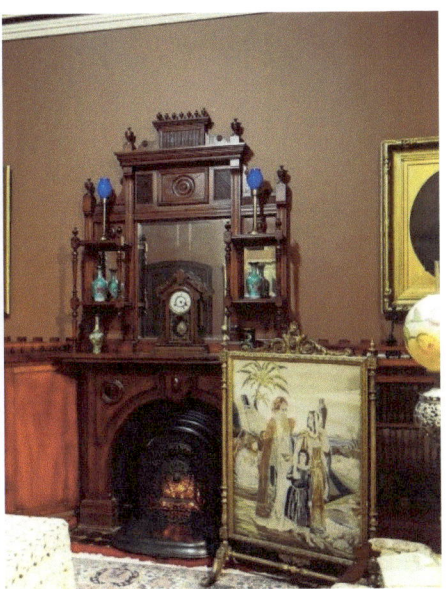

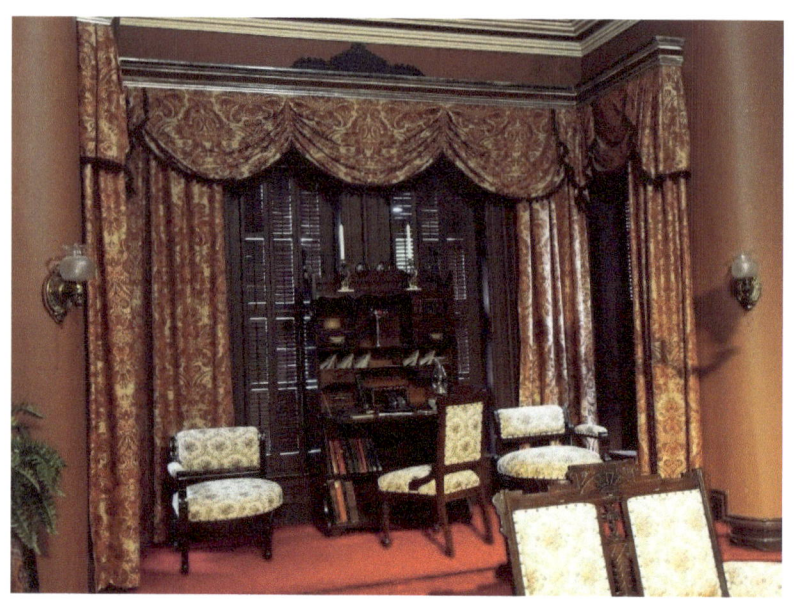

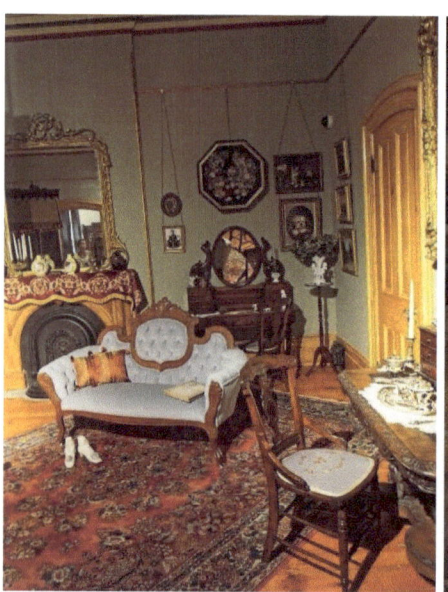

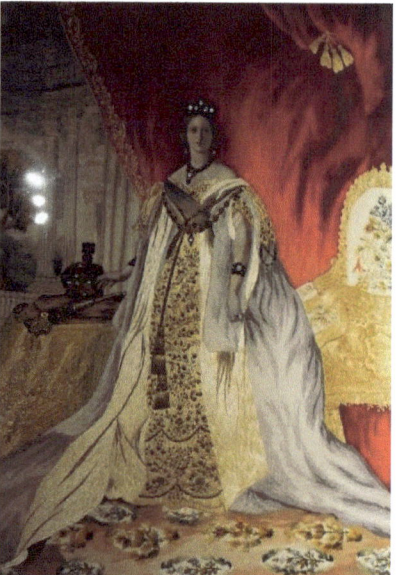

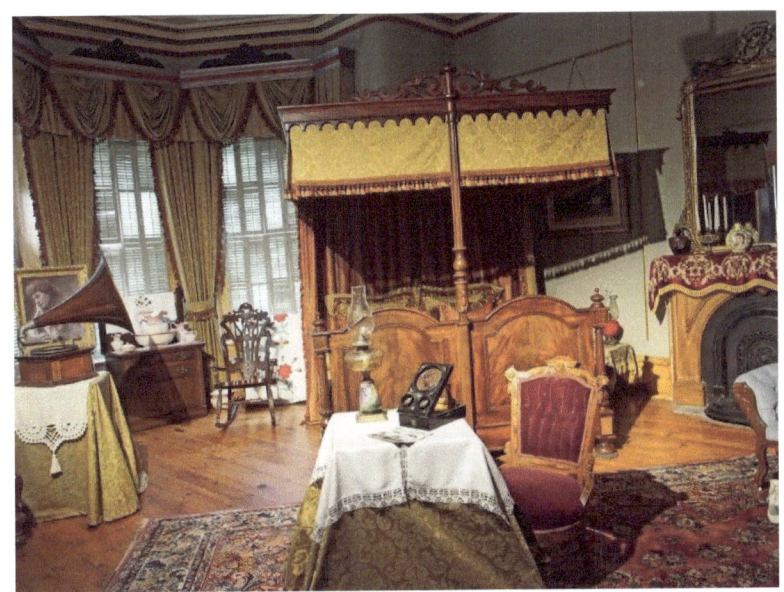

Master Bedroom

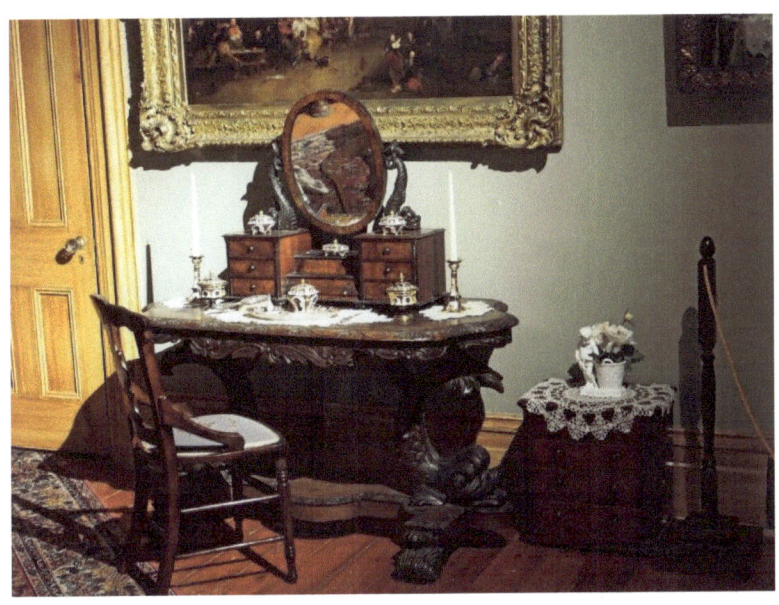

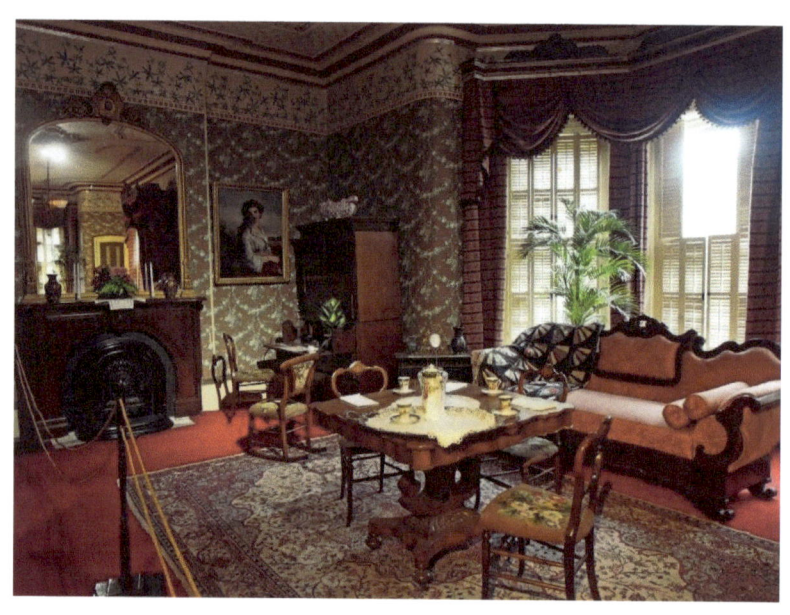

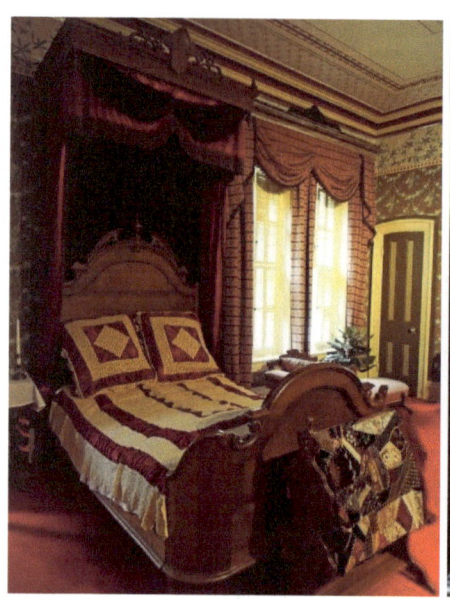

Spare Bedroom

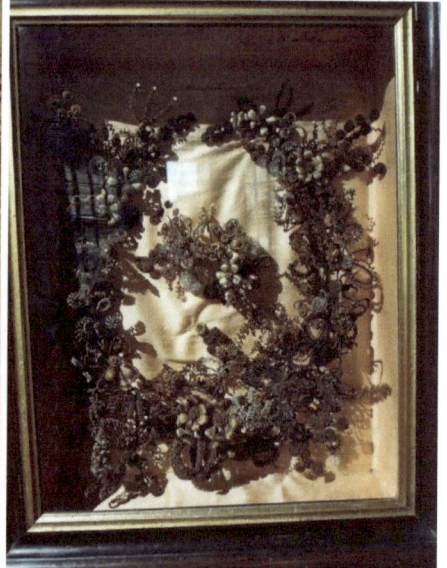

Hair Picture

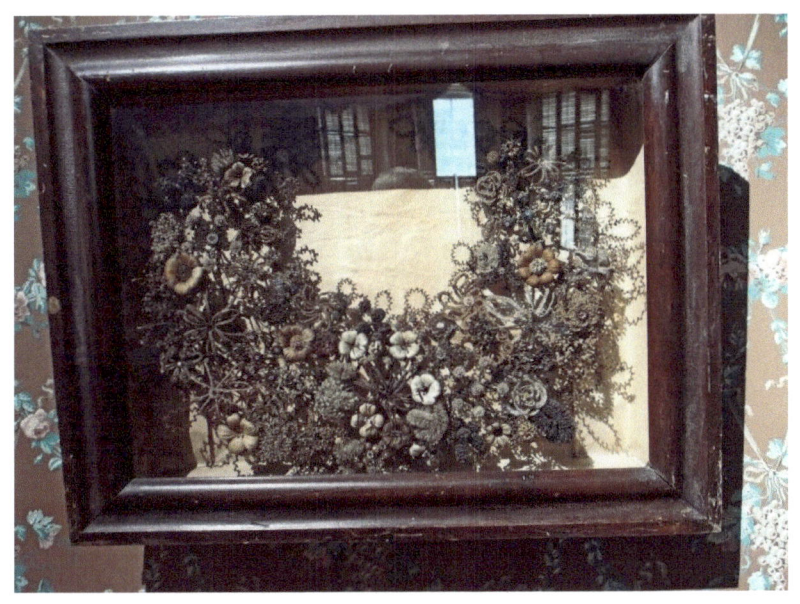

Hair pictures

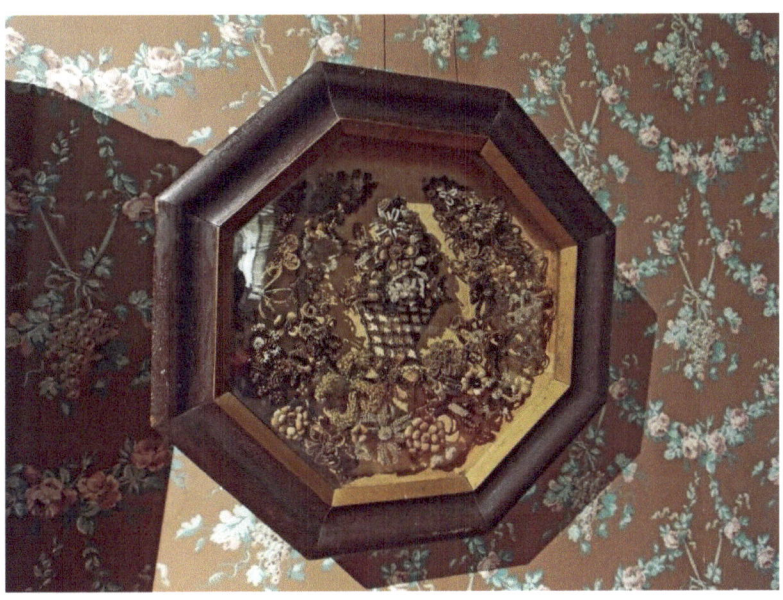

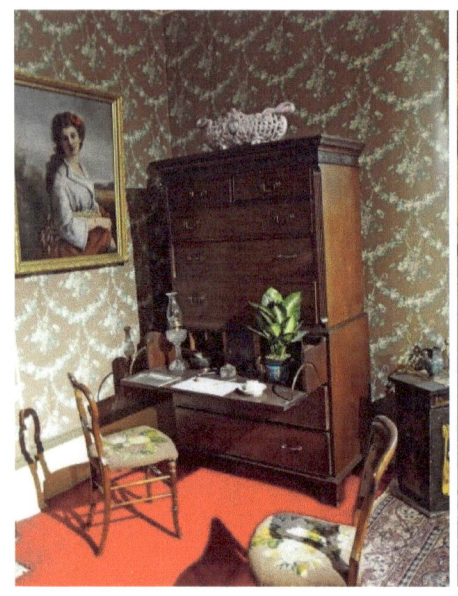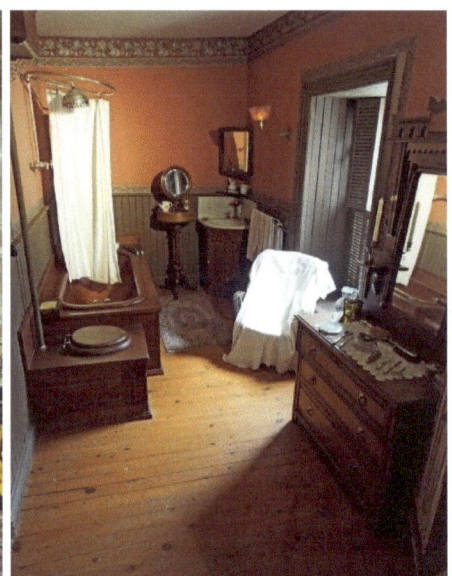

Bathroom

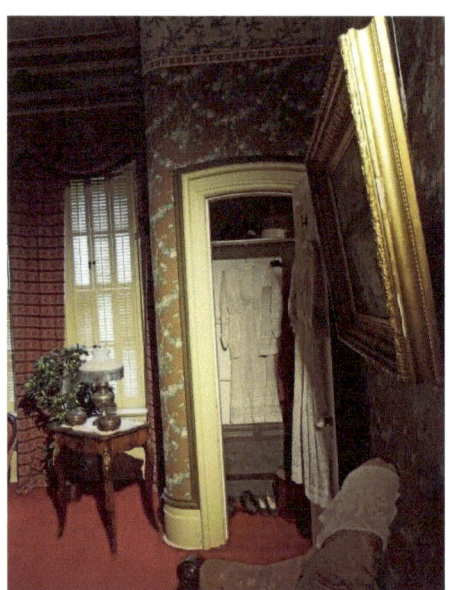

Closet

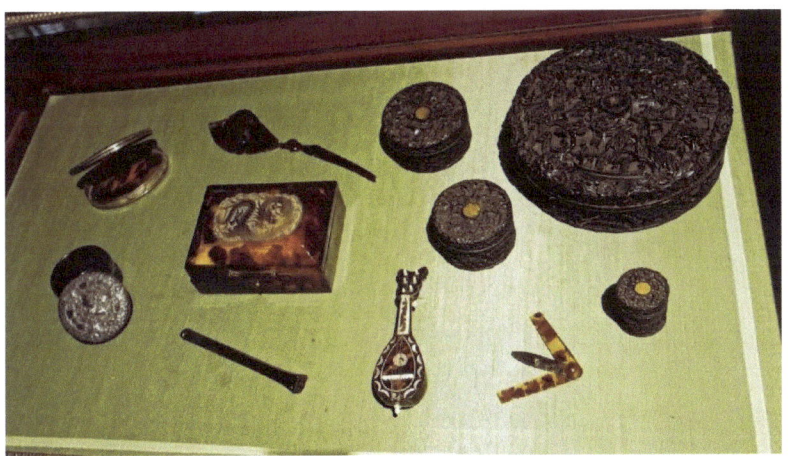

Tortoiseshell was used as an ornamental material in jewelry, musical instruments, furniture inlays, household items and other decorative pieces. Tortoiseshell was highly sought after because of its beautiful mottled patterns and variety of colors.

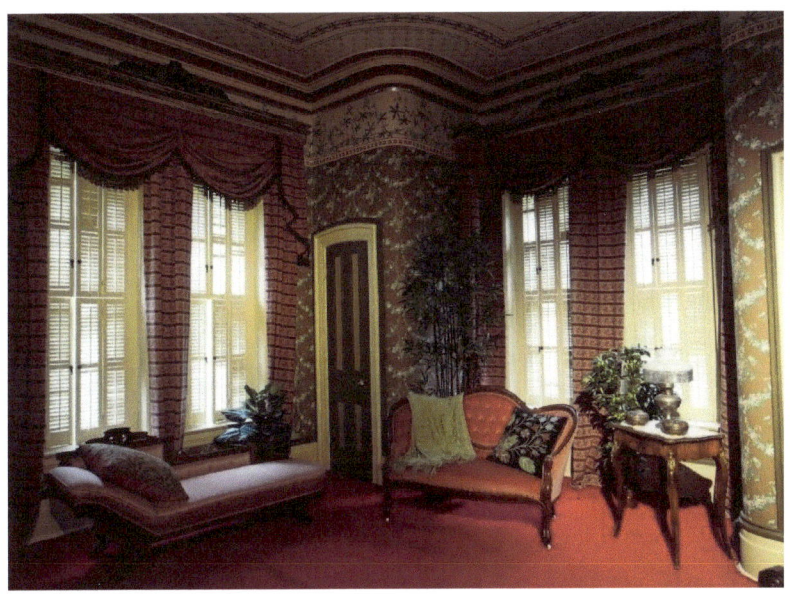

Paintings by Rev. Bowen P. Squire depicting aspects of Loyalist settlement in the Bay of Quinte region from 1784 to 1850

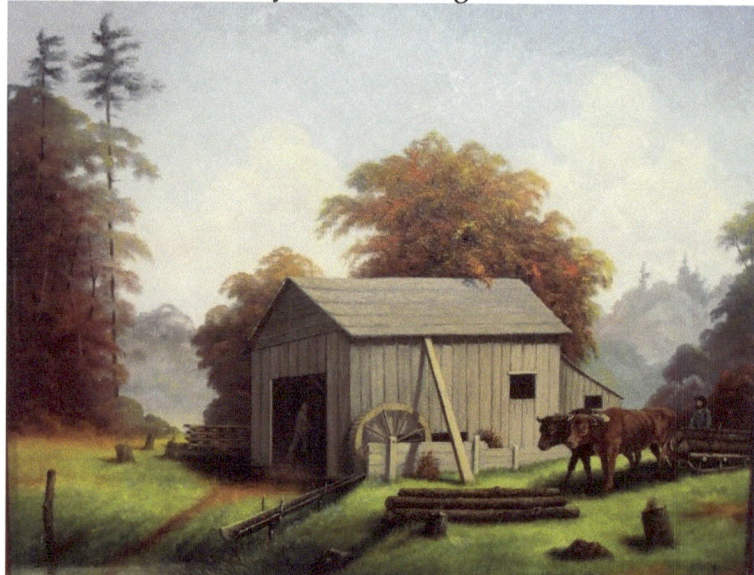

"The First Sawmill in Kente District" – the first sawmill was located in Millhaven. An undershot waterwheel ran the saw to cut lumber.

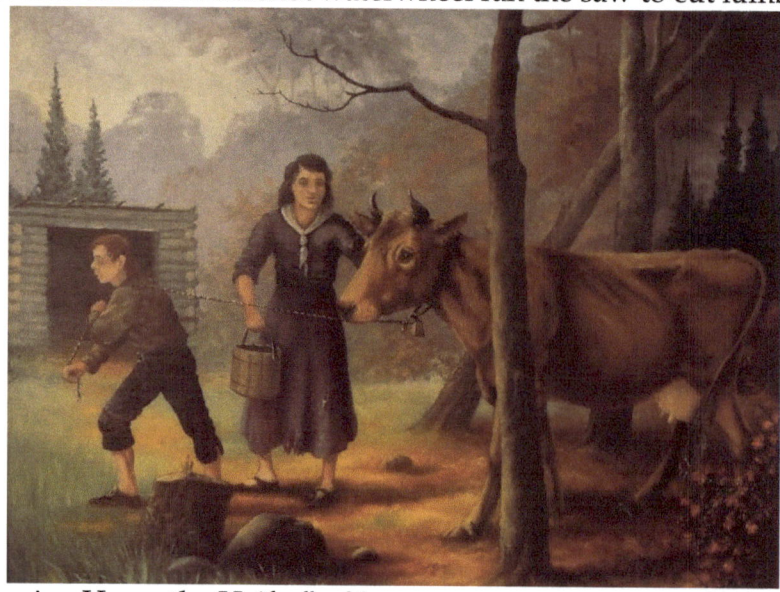

"Bringing Home the Heifer" – Young cows were sent out during the day to forage and brought home again in the evening.

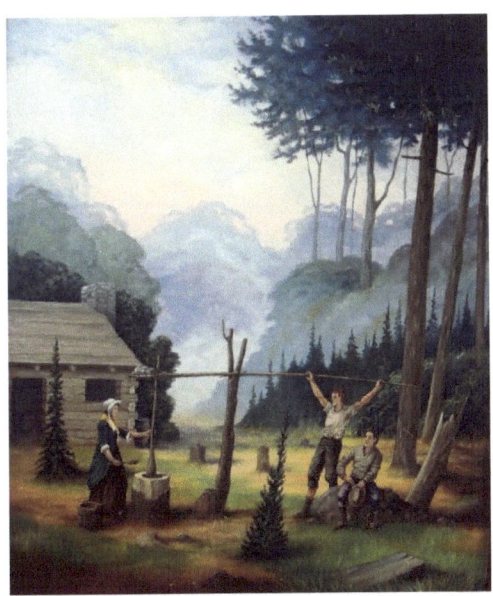

"Hominy Block" – Before grist mills were established, hominy (cracked corn) was made by pounding kernels into a coarse meal in a hollowed out hardwood stump. Most of the Loyalist settlers would grind or crush small quantities of corn for daily use.

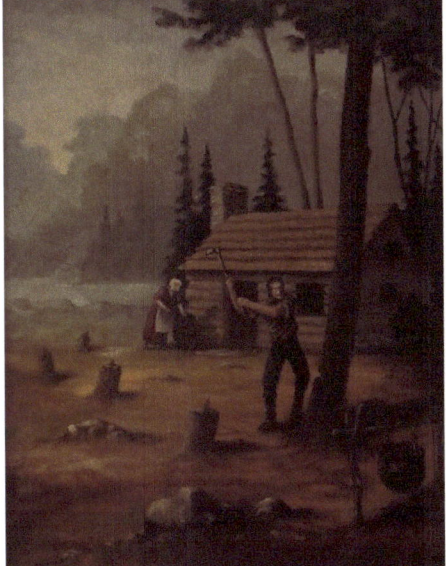

"100 Acres, an Axe, and a Kettle" – The Loyalists were granted land by the government and each family received an axe, kettle, some food, clothing and other supplies.

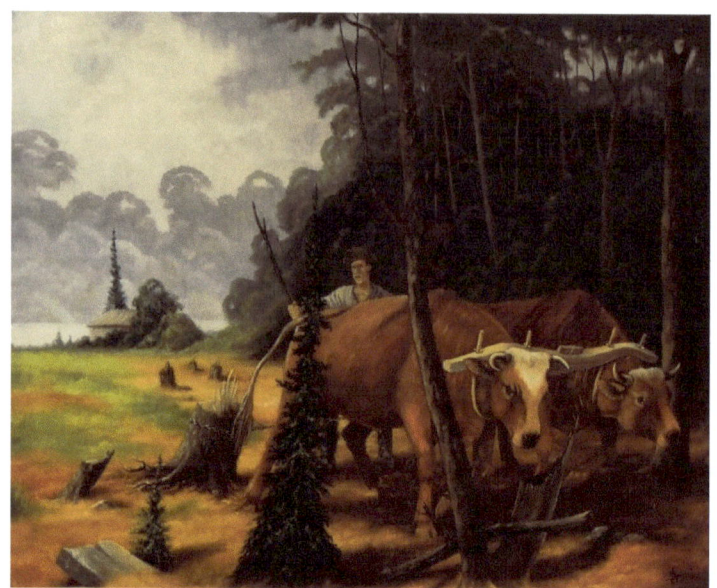

"Clearing the Land" – The settlers found that ashes from hardwood cleared from two acres of land would make three barrels of potash which was needed for making soap. This was the first "cash crop" for many settlers. It usually took a year, with help, to clear this much land.

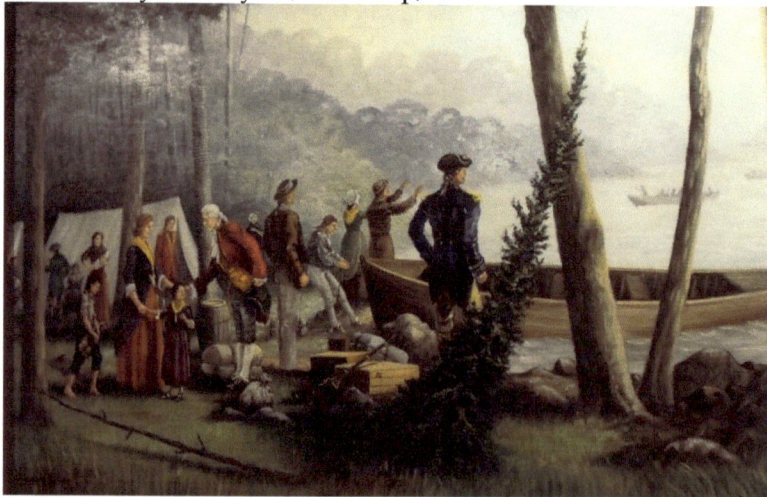

"Landing of the Loyalists" – On June 16, 1784 a group of United Empire Loyalists under Major Vanalstine landed at Adolphustown. They left New York in 1783, wintered in Sorel, Quebec, and travelled here in the spring by bateaux. Bateaux were large flat-bottomed boats suited to travel on the St. Lawrence River.

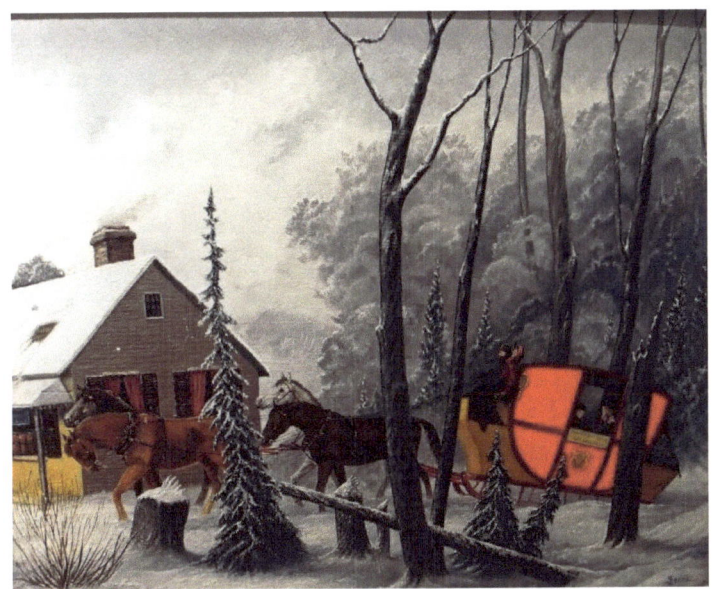

"Weller's Stagecoach" – Shown arriving at Finkle's Tavern in Bath c. 1820, this brightly colored vehicle with the king's coat-of-arms on the side was a common sight on the Kingston Road until the coming of the railroads. The fare from Kingston to York (Toronto) was six dollars.

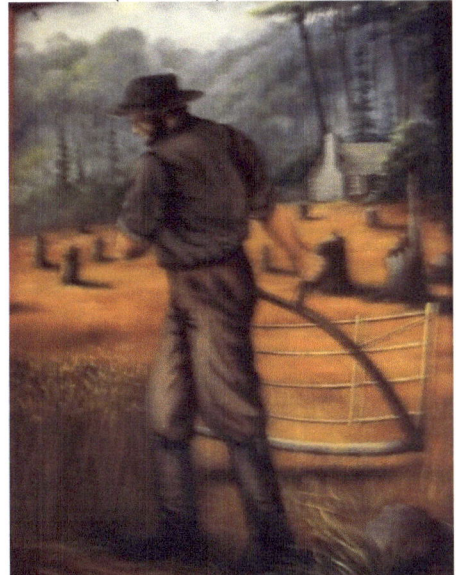

"Cradling Grain" – The pictures shows a man using a grain scythe in front of his homestead.

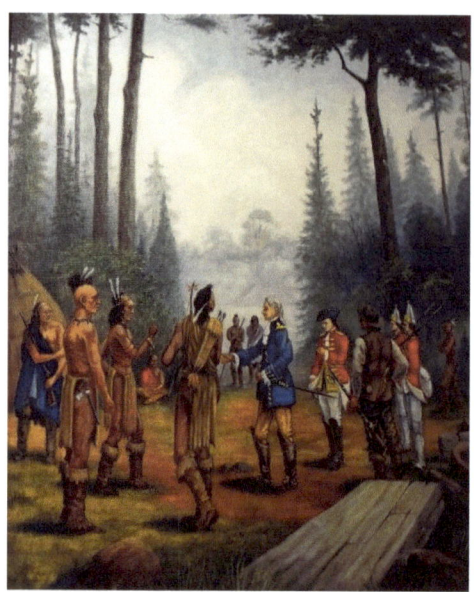

"Shotgun Treaty" portrays a meeting by Sir John Johnson from New York and the Mississauga Indians at the Carrying Place. The purpose of the meeting was to bargain lands for the Loyalist Iroquois (mainly Mohawk) who had been expelled from the United States following the Revolutionary War. In exchange for their land, the Mississaugas were given blankets, musket, shot, knives, and iron kettles. The arrangements were completed in 1897.

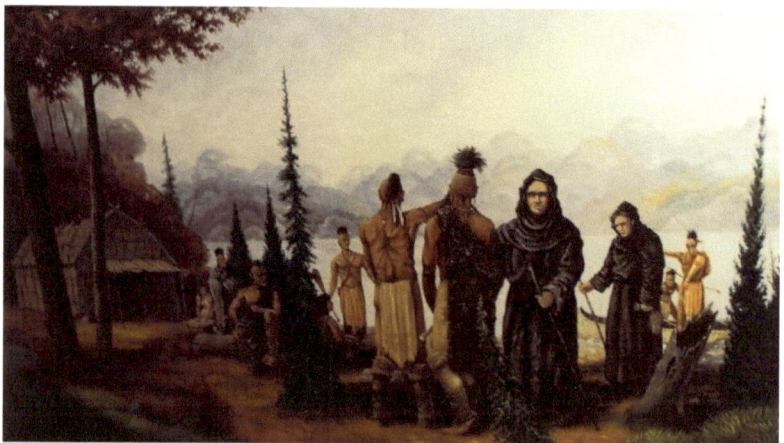

"The Landing of the Priests at Kente Village" – The Sulpicians were the first missionaries to visit the north shore of Lake Ontario in 1668. Later they were replaced by the Jesuits.

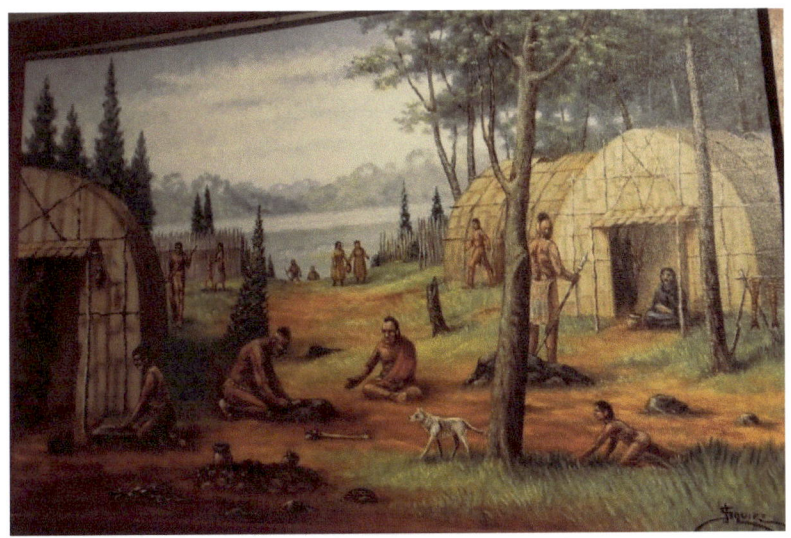

"Cayuga – Kente" – This painting depicts the Iroquois settlement at the Kente Mission site in Prince Edward County. Cayuga means village.

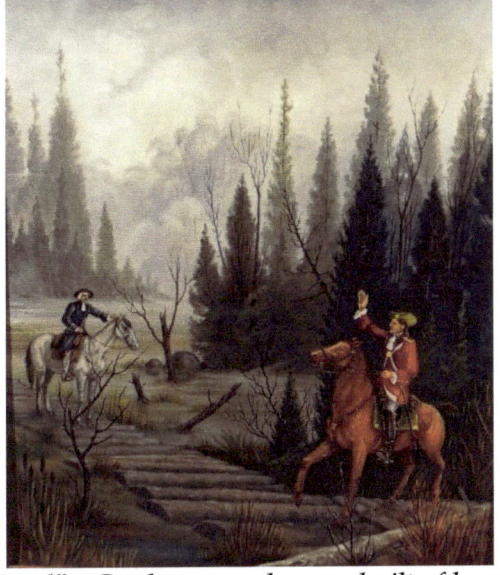

"The Corduroy Road" – Corduroy roads were built of logs split in half and placed flat side down, and were used especially in swampy areas. They were named after the ridged cloth in common use and noted for its durability. In this picture, set about 1788, the King's messenger meets the preacher: who will have the right of way?

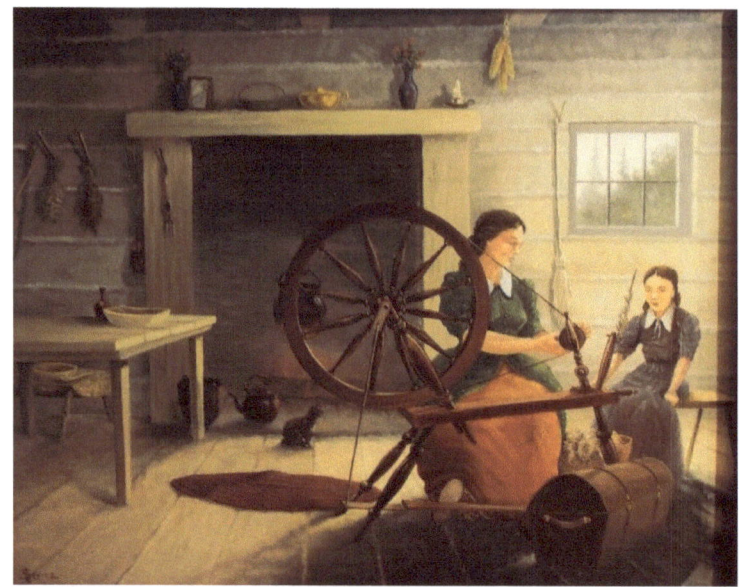

Spinning

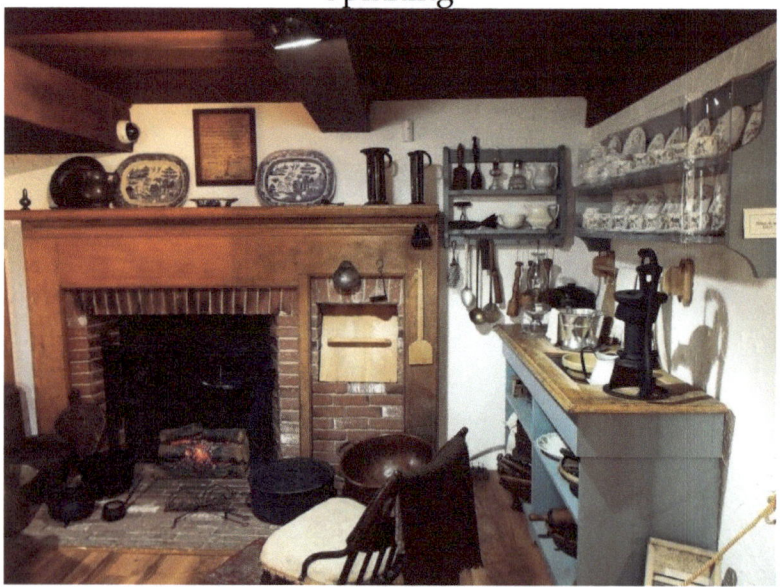

"Settler's Cabin" – This painting depicts the interior of an early settler's home. The first need of settlers was shelter, and instructions were given to them to build a log house twenty feet by thirty feet.

The dirt floor was packed down, a fireplace built, and the cracks between the logs filled with clay and moss. Windows were covered with glass or oiled skins. Once the door was hung, and the roof covered with bark, the house was ready for occupancy.

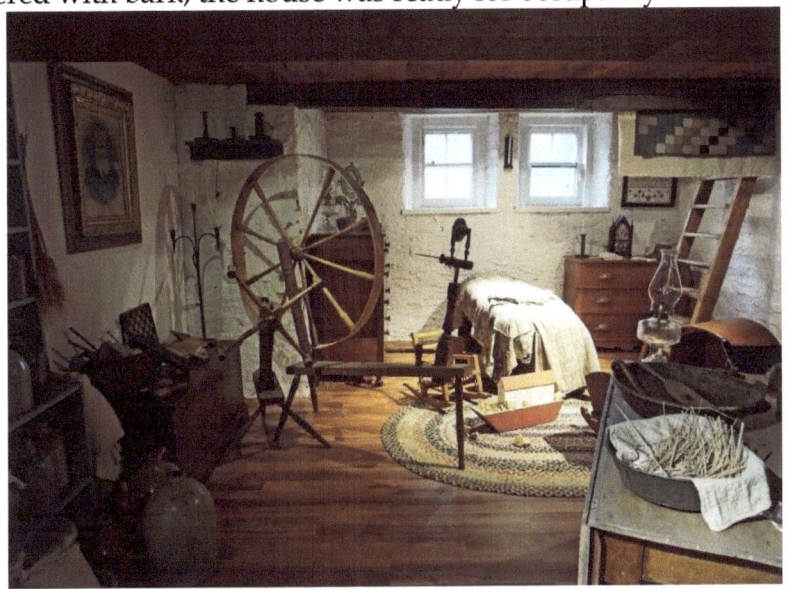

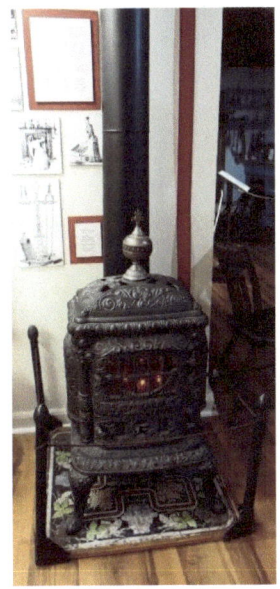
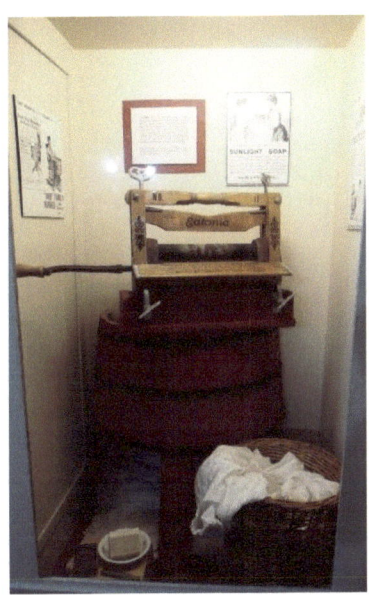

Stove   Laundry room

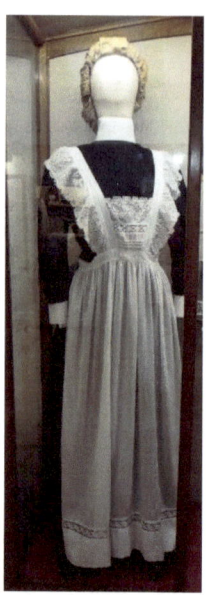

Maid of All Work uniform

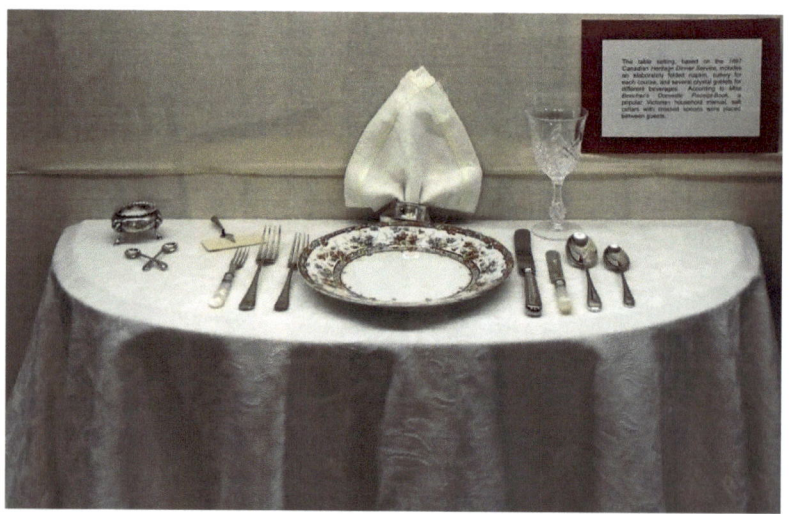

The Victorians were fond of elaborate and expensive table settings, with a wide range of formal tableware and serving pieces. These objects required polishing before any social gathering at Glanmore.

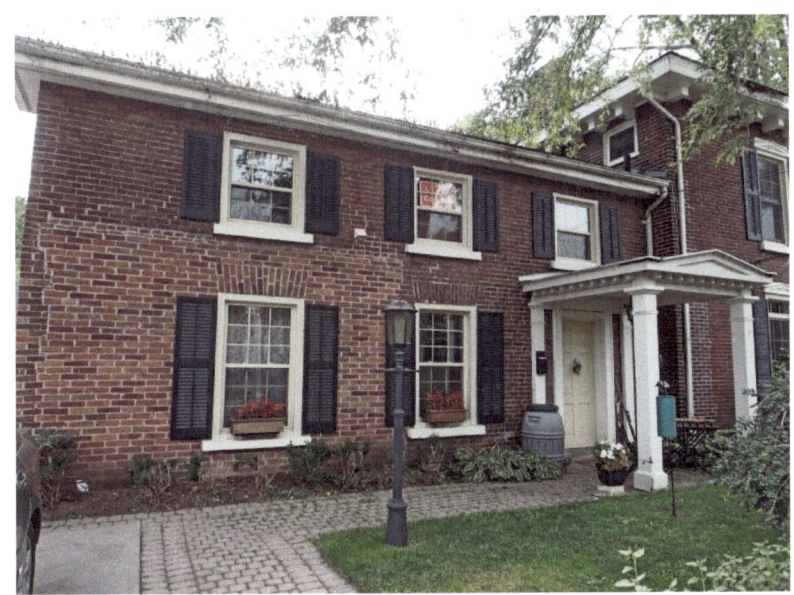

7 Queen Street

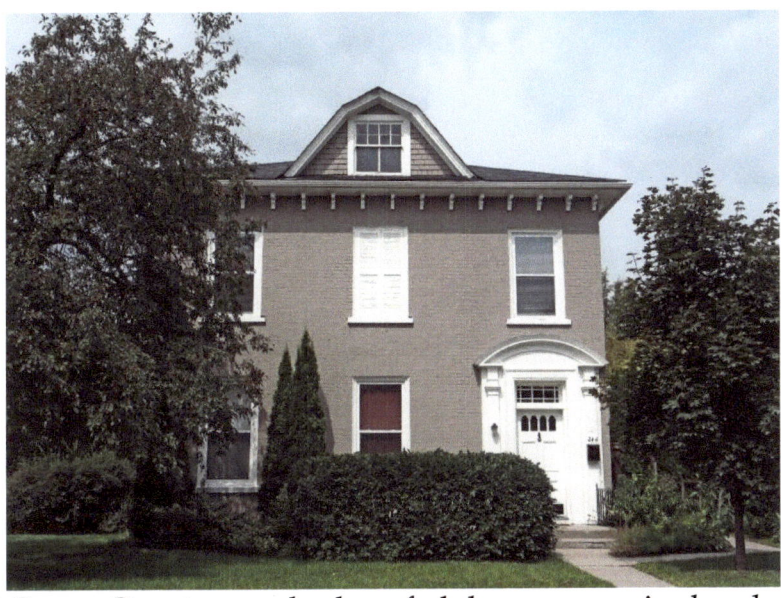

24 Queen Street – gambrel-roofed dormer; cornice brackets, engaged columns around entrance, transom window

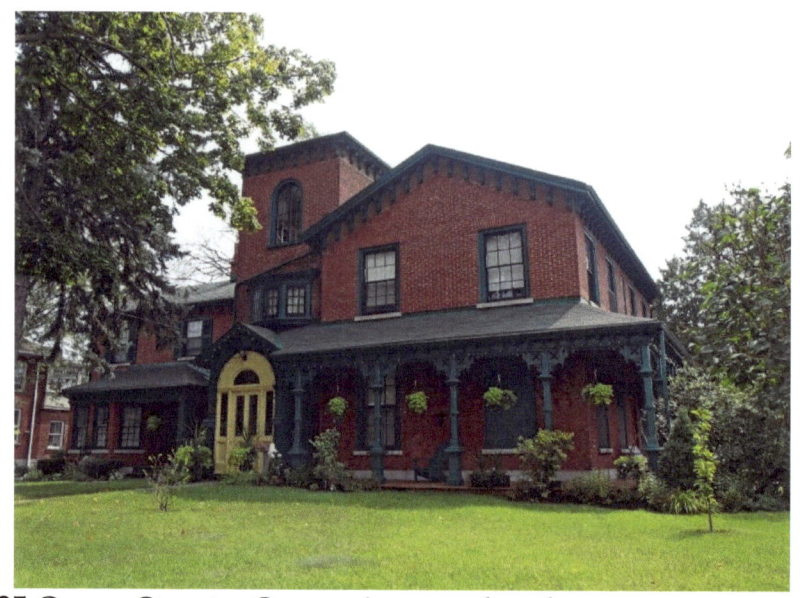

25 Queen Street – Queen Anne style - three-storey tower, cornice brackets, ornate capitals on the supports for the wraparound veranda

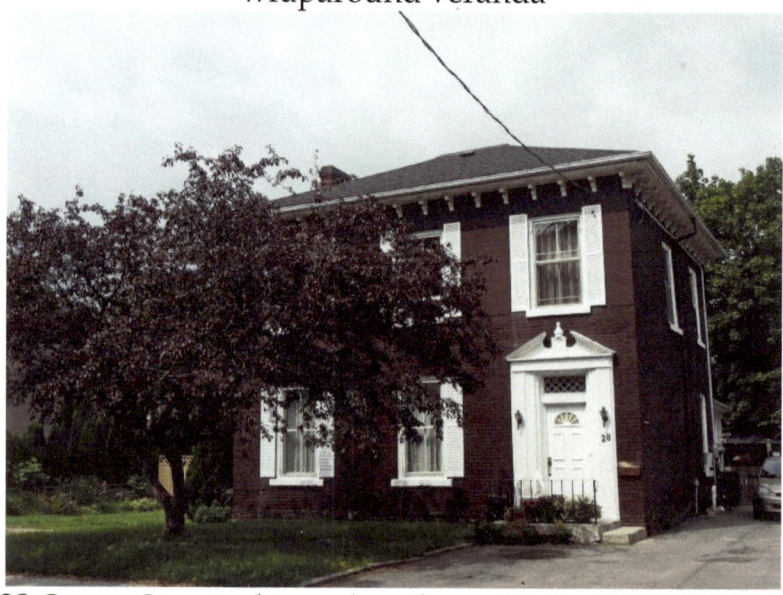

28 Queen Street – hipped roof, cornice brackets, broken pediment above door, transom window

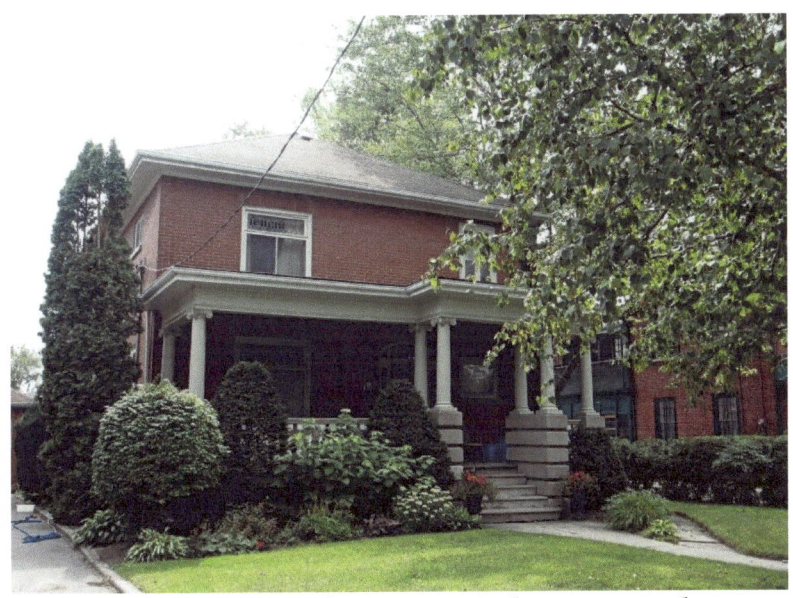

29 Queen Street – hip roof, Ionic capitals on veranda supports

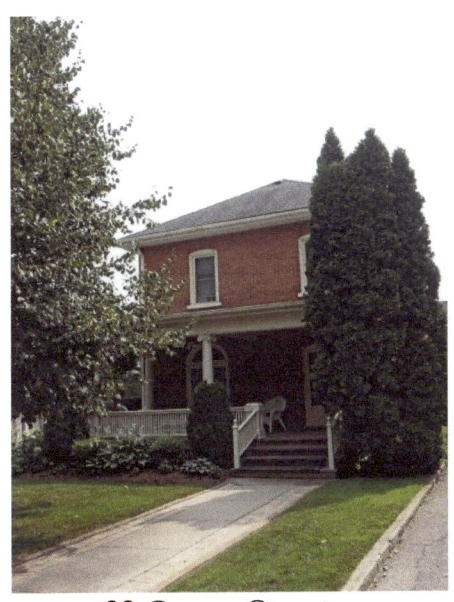

33 Queen Street
Hipped roof, Ionic capitals

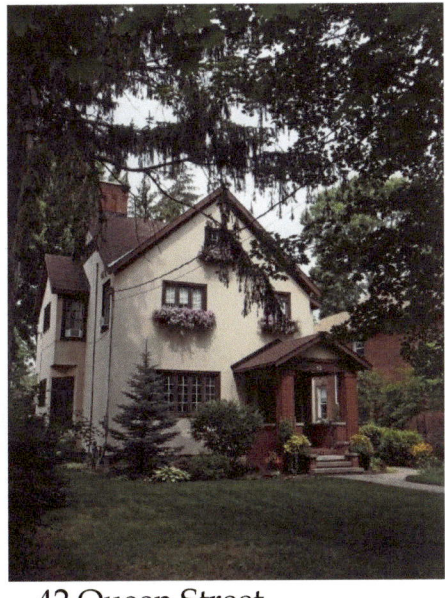

42 Queen Street
Gothic

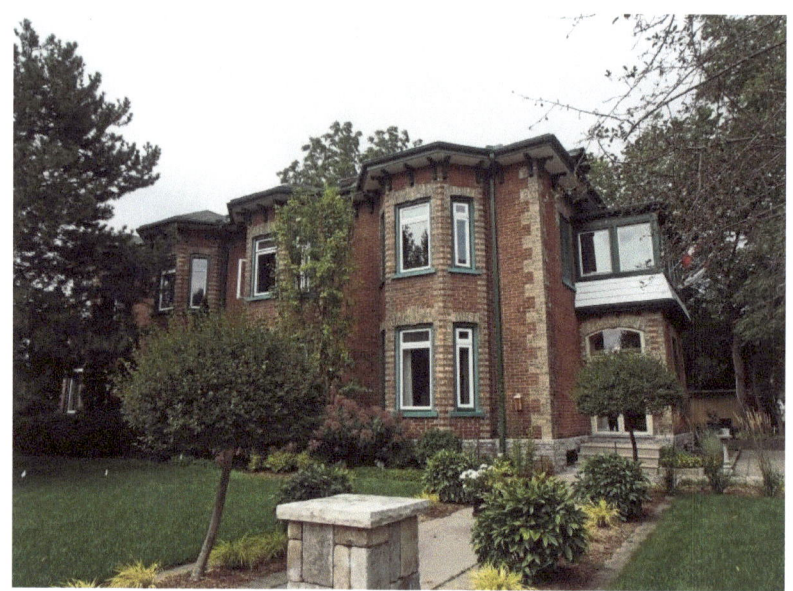

Queen Street – dichromatic brickwork, corner quoins, cornice brackets, two-storey bay windows

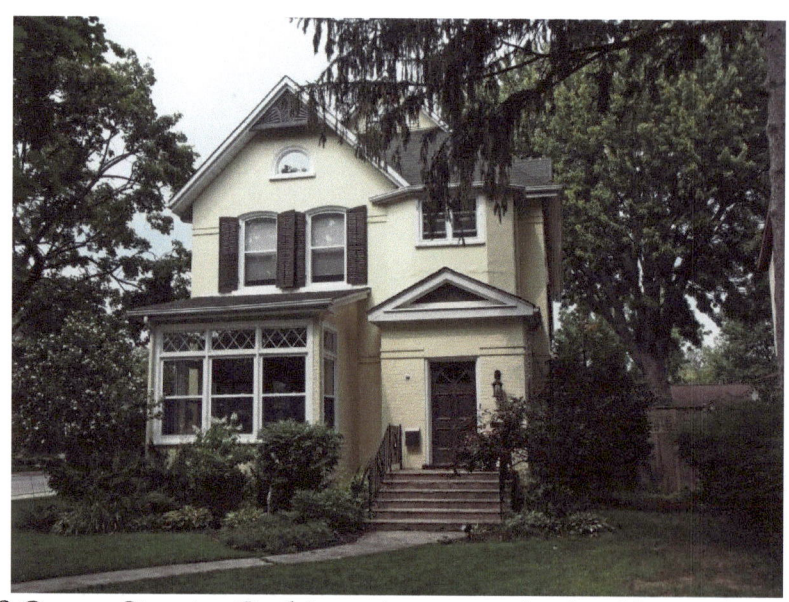

38 Queen Street – Gothic - trim on peak of gable, pediment

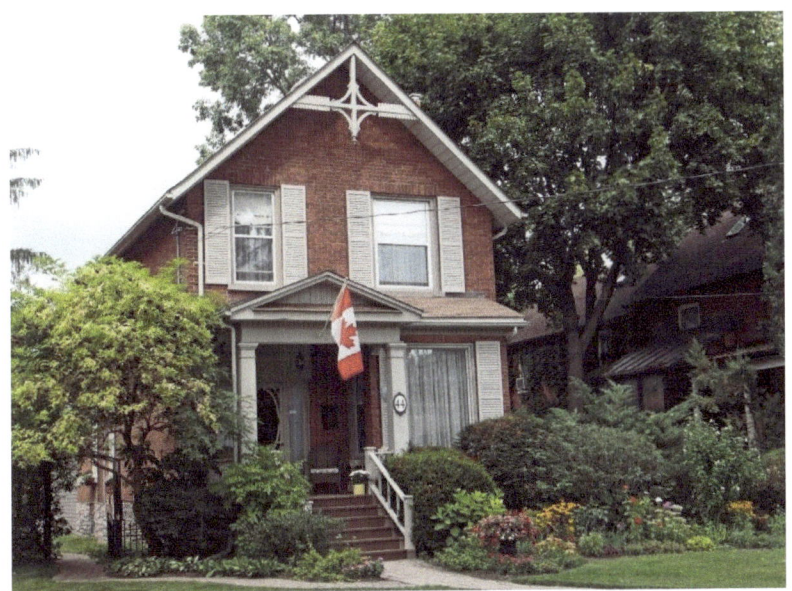

44 Queen Street – trim and finial on gable peak, pediment

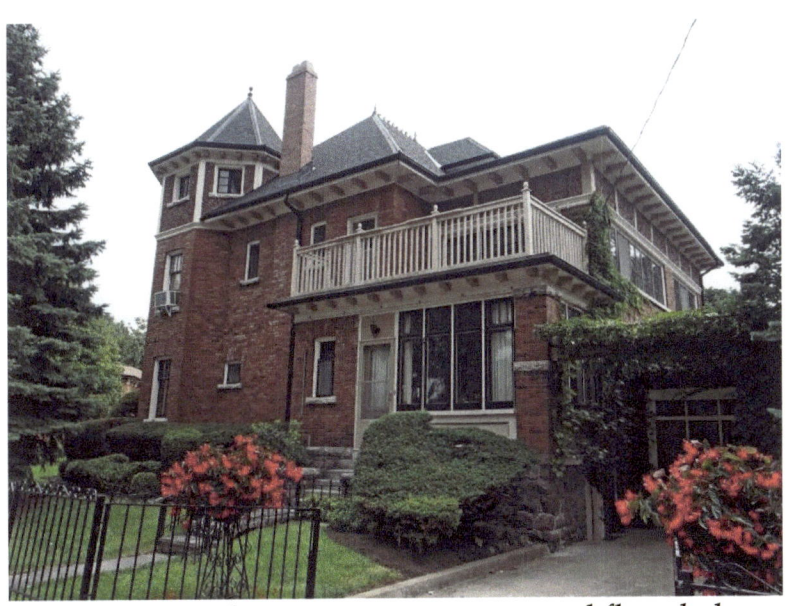

Queen Street – three-storey turret, second floor balcony

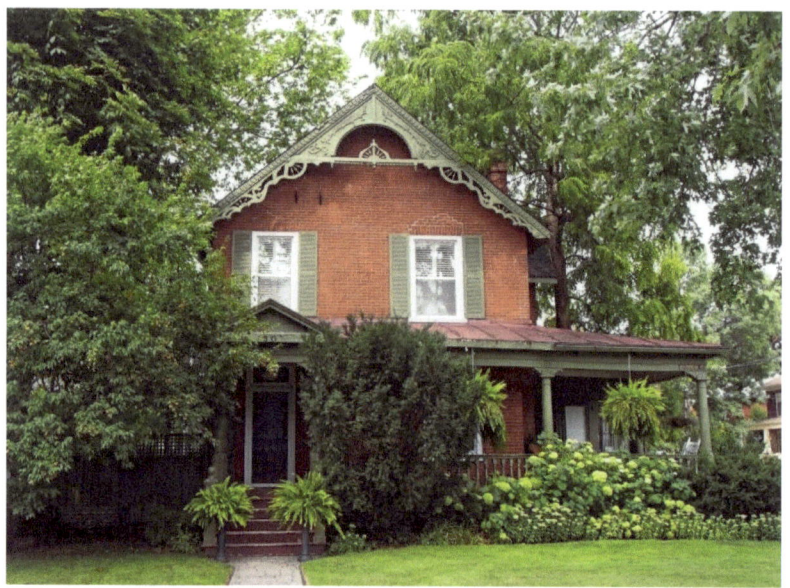

50 Queen Street – Gothic – verge board time on gable with decorative spindle work, pediment with decorated tympanum

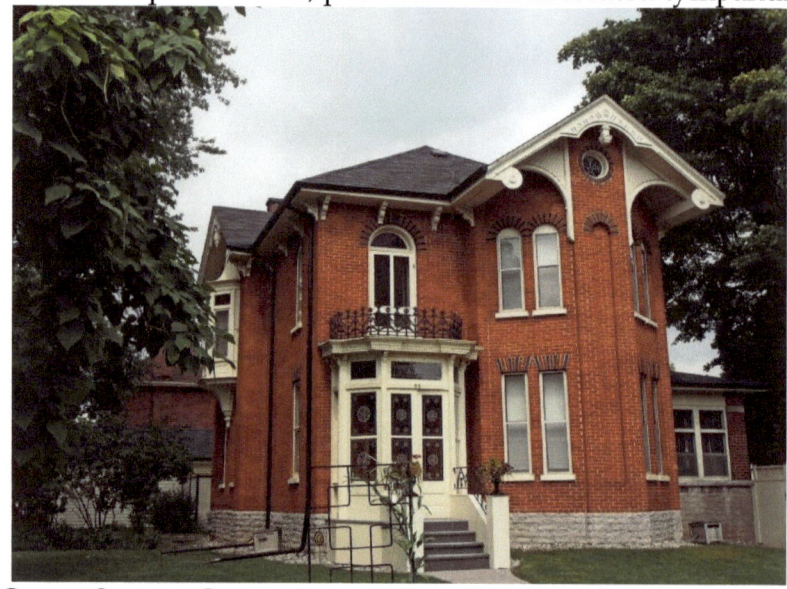

52 Queen Street – Queen Anne Villa – 2½-storey bay with trim and fretwork on gable; cornice brackets; bay window with iron cresting above, oriel window on side

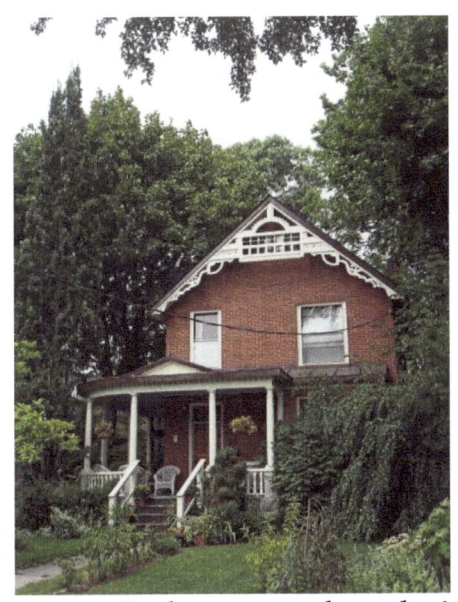

46 Queen Street – Gothic - verge board trim on gable

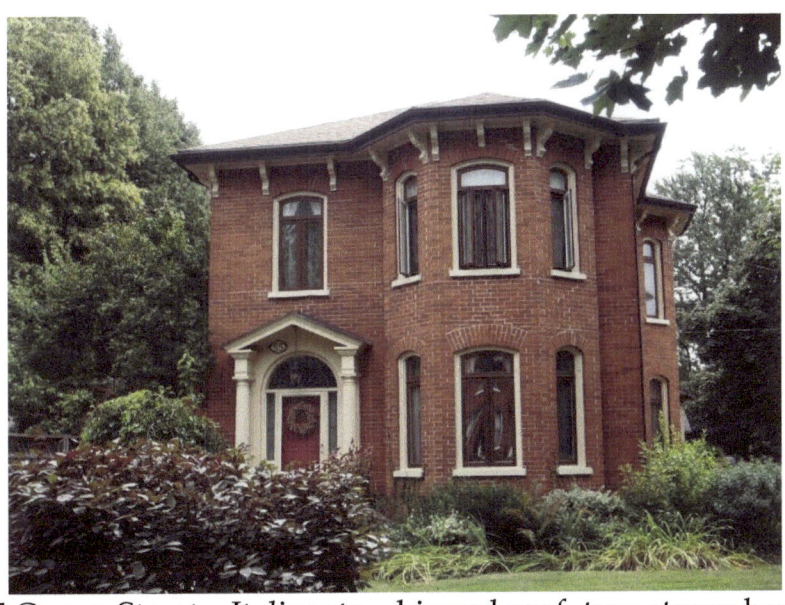

55 Queen Street – Italianate – hipped roof, two-storey bays, cornice brackets, Doric pillars with open pediment above, sidelights and transom window

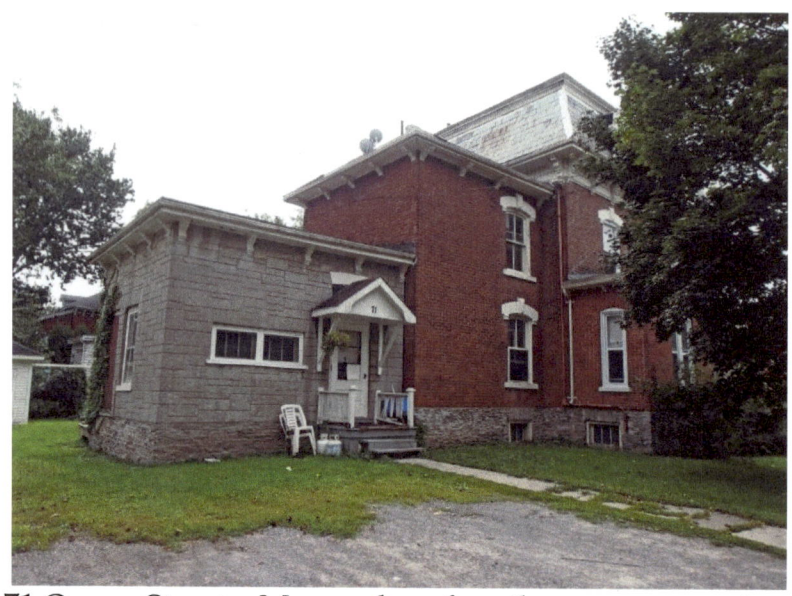

71 Queen Street – Mansard roof on three-storey section, cornice brackets

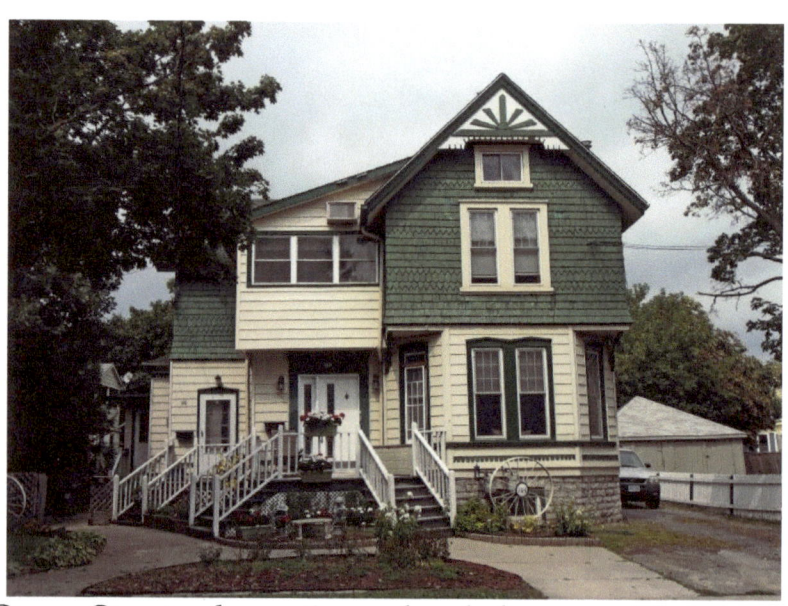

88 Queen Street – decorative cedar shakes on gable-face, verge board trim

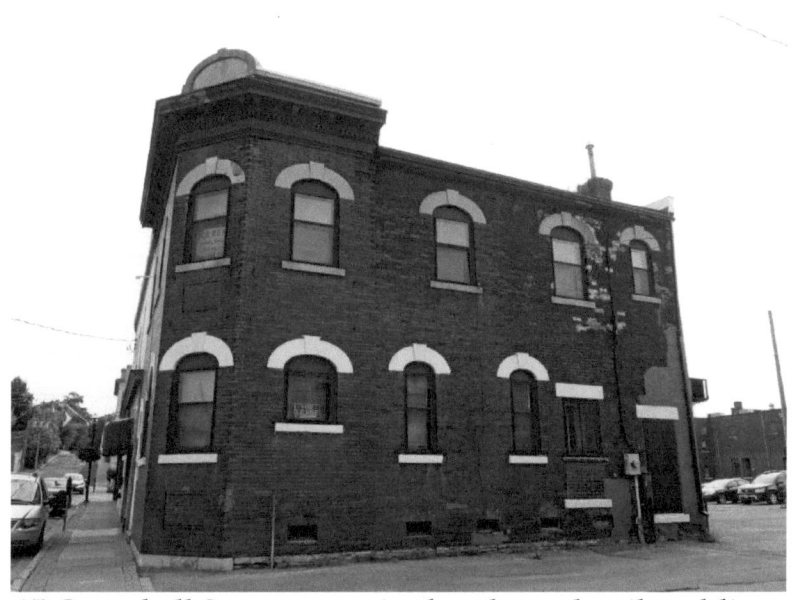

15 Campbell Street – cornice brackets, dentil molding, keystones

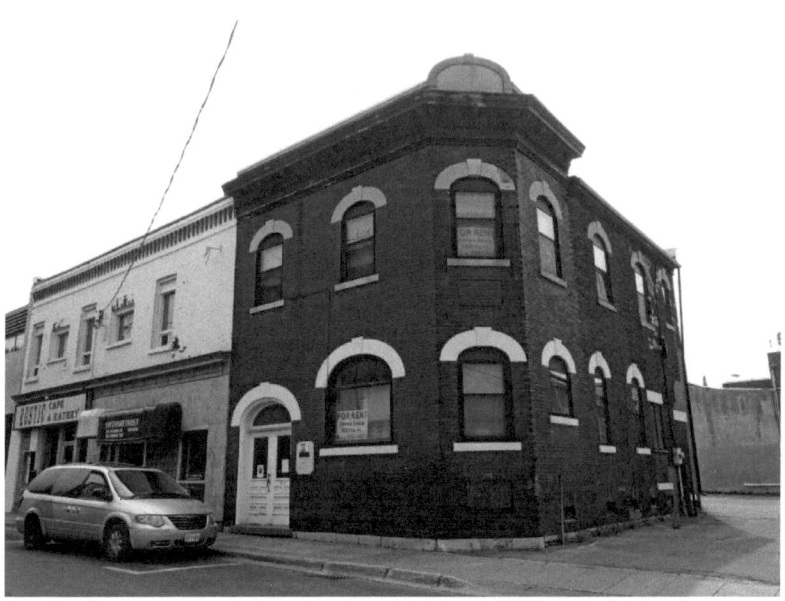

19 Campbell Street – 1909 – Rustic Café and Eatery

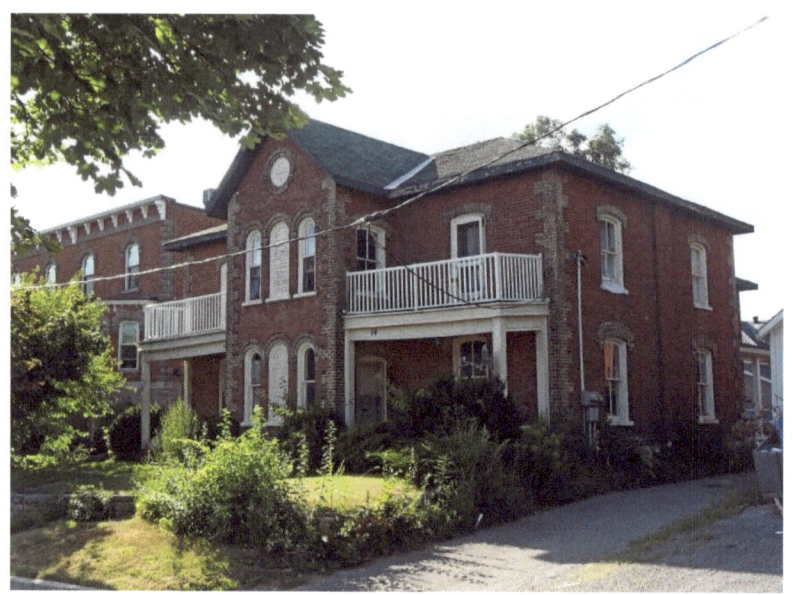

14 Patterson Avenue – dichromatic voussoirs and quoins, second floor balconies

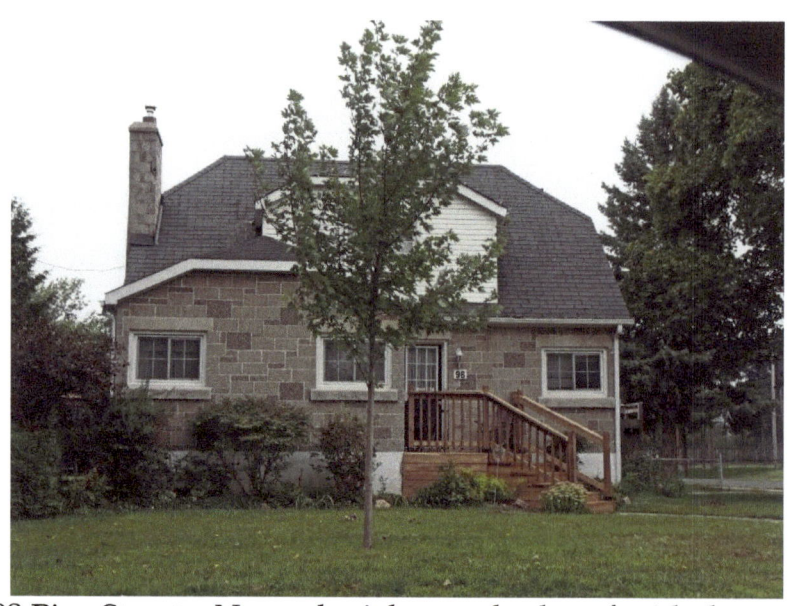

98 Pine Street – Neo-colonial – gambrel roof with dormer

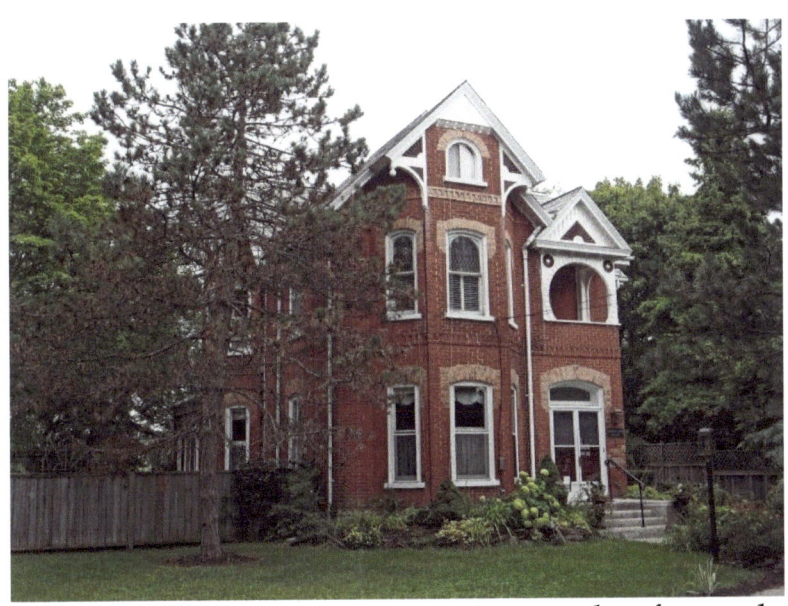

4 Pine Street – Crestview – Queen Anne style – fretwork on gable, pediment above semi-circular balcony opening, dichromatic voussoirs and dentil molding

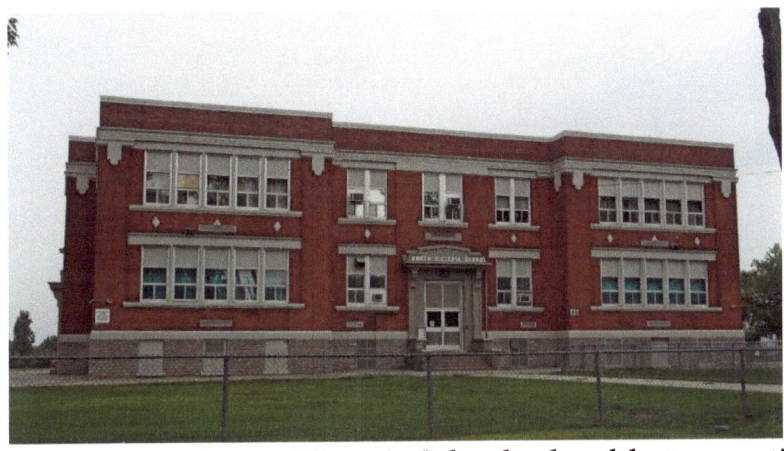

46 Pine Street – Queen Victoria School - the oldest operating school in Belleville, located on the east side of the Moira River, serves approximately 300 students from Junior Kindergarten to Grade 6

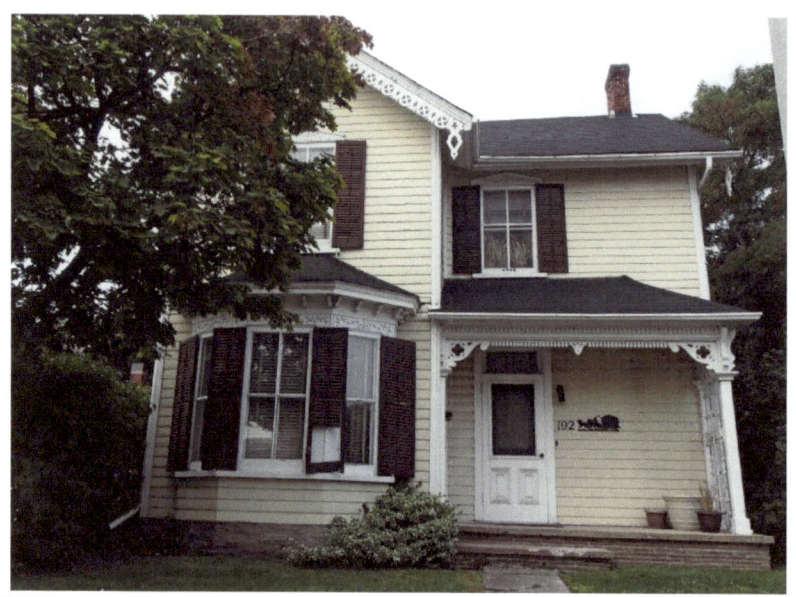

192 James Street – Gothic – verge board trim on gable, bay window, bric-a-brac on veranda

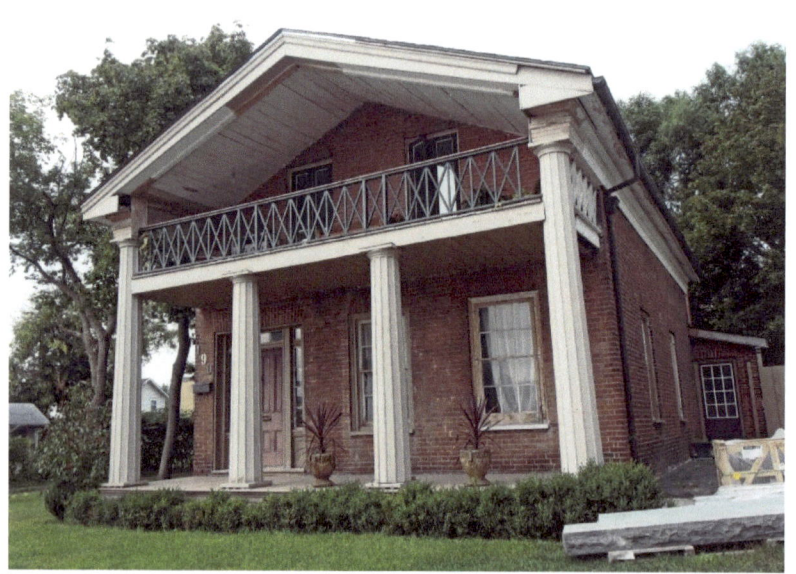

190 James Street – second floor balcony with tall supporting pillars

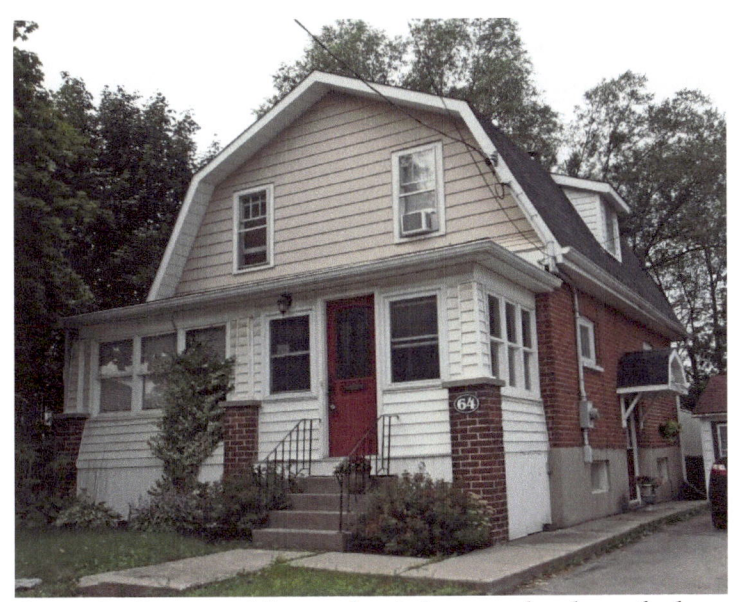

64 Octavia Street – Neo-colonial – gambrel roof, dormer

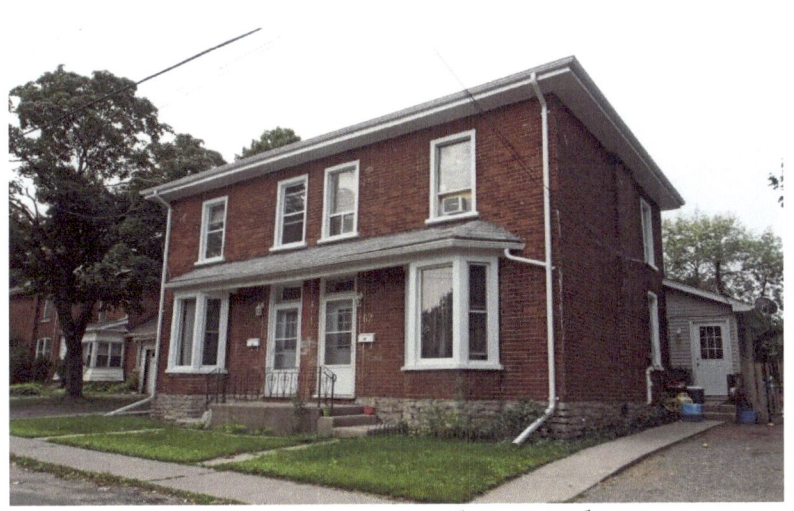

60-62 Octavia Street – bay windows

Architectural Terms

Banding: Different materials, colors or textures used in horizontal bands along a wall. Example: 105 Bridge Street East, Page 10	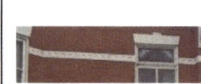
Bay Window: A window that projects out from a wall, in a semicircular, rectangular, or polygonal design. Used frequently in Gothic and Victorian designs. Example: 60-62 Octavia Street, Page 59	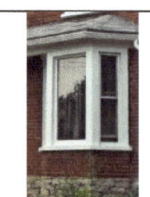
Brackets: a decorative or weight-bearing structural element which forms a right angle with one side against a wall and the other under a projecting surface such as an eave or roof. Example: 257 Bridge Street East, Page 16	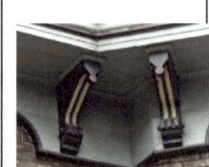
Capital: The uppermost finish or decoration on a column. An Ionic column has a small base, a thin elegant shaft, and a capital composed of volutes which are carved whirls or twists that take the form of a scroll. Example: 29 Queen Street, Pg. 49 A Doric column is characterized by a plain column with no base, a shaft with twenty flutings, and a simple capital with a simple entablature. Example: Bridge Street East, Page 9 A Corinthian column is characterized by a rounded capital decorated with acanthus leaves and a square abacus (the uppermost portion of a capital directly below the entablature) on tall slender columns. Example: 105 Bridge Street East, Page 10	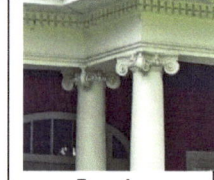 Ionic 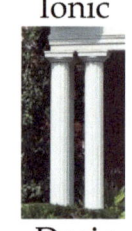 Doric 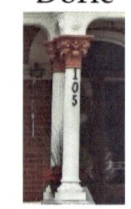 Corinthian

A Composite column is a mixture of two or three, of the major styles of Ionic, Doric and Corinthian. Example: 257 Bridge Street East, Page 26	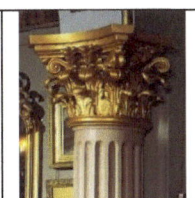
Cornice: originally the wooden overhang of the roof. With the use of stone, brick, iron and steel, the cornice is any horizontal moulded projection at the top of a building. They can be very decorative. Example: 34 Bridge.Street East, Page 6	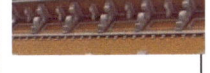
Cornice Return: decorative element on the end of a gable. Example: 105 Bridge Street East, Page 10	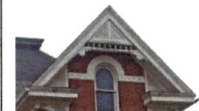
Dentil Moulding: an even series of rectangles used as ornamental decoration in cornices. Example: corner of Pinnacle Street, Page 8	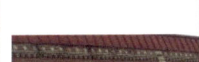
Dichromatic brickwork: the use of two colours of brick, tile or slate to decorate a façade. Polychromatic is the use of more than two colours. Example: 257 Bridge Street East, Page 16	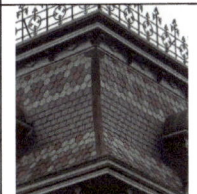
Dormer: (French for "sleep") a gable end window that pierces through the plane of a sloping roof surface to create usable space in the top floor or attic of a building by adding headroom. Example: 126 Bridge Street East, Page 14	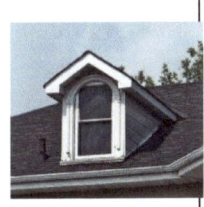

Gable: the triangular portion of a wall between the edges of a sloping roof. Example: 122 Bridge Street East, Page 14	
Gambrel Roof: a symmetrical two-sided roof with two slopes on each side; the upper slope is positioned at a shallow angle, while the lower slope is steep. It is similar to a mansard roof, but a gambrel has vertical gable ends instead of being hipped at the four corners of the building. Example: 64 Octavia Street, Page 59	
Hipped Roof: a roof where all sides slope downwards to the walls with no gables. Example: Bridge Street East, Page 9	
Iron Cresting: A decorative ornament along the top of a roof. Iron cresting was popular in the Baroque era and also in Italianate, Victorian, Second Empire and Queen Anne styles of architecture. Example: 257 Bridge Street East, Page 16	
Keystones and Voussoirs: a voussoir is a wedge-shaped element used in building an arch. A keystone is the central stone that locks all the stones into position, allowing the arch to bear weight. A keystone is often enlarged and embellished. Example: 15 Campbell (keystones), Page 55 4 Pine Street (voussoirs), Page 57	 keystone voussoirs

Mansard Roof: This style was popularized by Francois Mansart (1598-1666), an accomplished architect of the French Baroque period and especially fashionable during the Second French Empire (1852-1870). This roof is almost flat on the top section, with two slopes on each of its sides with the lower slope at a steeper angle than the upper, and has dormer windows. Example: 257 Bridge Street East, Page 16	
Muntin: When a window unit has more than one pane, the material that separates the panes is called the muntin. The larger, more decorative separations are called mullions. In stained glass windows, each piece of colored glass is held in place by a muntin. These were traditionally made of iron. Example: 60 Bridge Street East, Page 8	
Pediment: a triangular section above the door or portico, usually supported by columns. The inside of the triangle is called the tympanum. Example: 28 Queen Street, Page 48	
Pilaster: a slightly projecting column built into or applied to the face of a wall for additional structural support. Example: corner of Pinnacle Street, Page 8	

Quoin: masonry blocks at the corner of a wall, often a decorative feature, usually larger or of a different colour than the rest of the wall. Example: Queen Street, Page 50	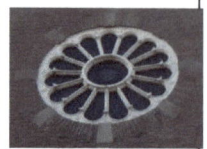
Rose Window: a circular window with ornamental tracery radiating from the centre. Example: 60 Bridge Street East, Page 8	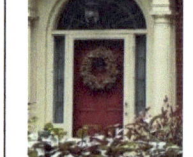
Sidelight: a vertical window that flanks a door, and is often used to emphasize the importance of a primary entrance. **Transom Window:** the light above the doorway, also called a fanlight. Example: 55 Queen Street, Page 53	
Tower: A circular, square, or octagonal vertical structure higher than the surrounding structure that is usually part of an existing building and is created either for extra defense or for a specific purpose such as a clock or a bell tower. Example: Bridge Street East, Page 7	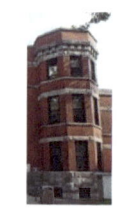

Turret: a small tower that projects from the wall of a building. Example: 128 Bridge Street East, Page 15	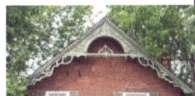
Verge board and Finial: also called bargeboards – hang from the projecting end of a roof and are often elaborately carved and ornamented. **Finial:** ornament added to the top of a gable, pinnacle, canopy or spire – a Gothic element. Example: 50 Queen Street, Page 52	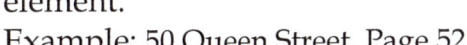

Gothic Revival, 1830-1890 – These decorative buildings have sharply-pitched gables with highly detailed verge boards, pointed-arch window openings, and dichromatic brickwork. It is a common style in Ontario. Example: 50 Queen Street, Page 52	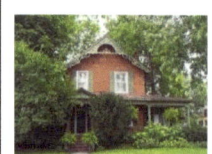
Italianate, 1850-1900 – A two story rectangular building with a mild hip roof, a projecting frontispiece, and generous eaves with ornate cornice brackets was the basis of the style; often there are large sash windows, quoins, ornate detailing on the windows, belvederes and wraparound verandahs. Italianate commercial buildings often have cast iron cresting and elegant window surrounds. Example: 105 Bridge Street East, Page 10	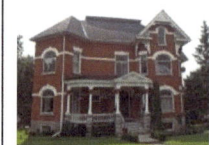
Queen Anne, 1885-1900 – This style is distinguished by an irregular outline featuring a combination of an offset tower, broad gables, projecting two-storey bays, verandahs, multi-sloped roofs, and tall, decorative chimneys. A mixture of brick and wood is common. Windows often have one large single-paned bottom sash and small panes in the upper sash. Example: 128 Bridge Street East, Page 15	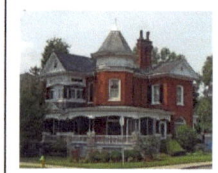

Neo-colonial (also Colonial Revival, Georgian Revival or Neo-Georgian) architecture seeks to revive elements of architectural style of American colonial architecture of the period around the Revolutionary War which drew strongly from Georgian architecture of Great Britain. Architecture from the 18th and early 19th centuries in Ontario includes a wide assortment of detailing and ornament applied to a design centered around the fireplace and the source of water. Structures are typically two stories, have a symmetrical front facade with elaborate front doorways, often with decorative crown pediments, fanlights, and sidelights, symmetrical windows flanking the front entrance, often in pairs or threes, and columned porches. Example: 64 Octavia Street, Page 59	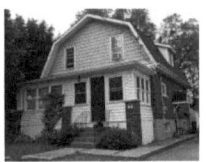
Second Empire, 1860-1880 – The mansard roof is the most noteworthy feature of this style and is evidence of the French origins. Projecting central towers and one or two-storey bays can also be present. Example: 257 Bridge Street East, Page 16	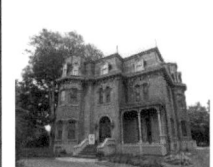

www.ingramcontent.com/pod-product-compliance
Lightning Source LLC
Chambersburg PA
CBHW040841180526
45159CB00001B/273